BANCHETTI

Cooking Renaissance Italian Food

51 Redacted Recipes from the 1549 *Banchetti*

by Christoforo Messisbugo

Translated and Redacted by Master Basilius Phocas
(Charles A. Potter)

CuMhara Publishing
Morning View, Kentucky

Copyright © 2023

You may use or distribute this work for
non-profit use only (scholarly, private use)
provided that proper attributions are given.

My e-mail is basiliusphocas@hotmail.com

Charles Potter

ISBN:
9798392237593

In loving memory of

Angela Christina Cropley

BANCHETTI

COMPOSITIONI DI
VIVANDE, ET AP-
PARECCHIO GE-
NERALE, DI
CHRISTOFORO
DI MESSI-
SBVGO.

ALLO ILLVSTRISSIMO
ET REVERENDISSIMO
SIGNOR IL SIGNOR
DON HIPPOLITO
DA ESTE,
CARDINALE DI
FERRARA.

Con gratia  Et Priuilegio.

IN FERRARA, PER GIOVANNI
De Buglhat Et Antonio Hucher Compagni.
Nell'Anno. M. D. XLIX.

Table of Contents

Introduction   1
     Libro Novo menu in the middle of August 1530
     Dinner on the eighth of September 1531
     Ingredients for Cooking Italian Renaissance
     Italian weights and measures from the Middle Ages to the Nineteenth Century

Chapter 1   **Compositone Della Piu Importanti Vivande**   20
               (Composition of the Most Important Foods)

     1A   To First Make Fifty Breads of Milk and Sugar
     1B   Bagels of Milk and Sugar
     1C   To Make Thirty Six of the Most Perfect Cookies
     4C   To Make Ten Wreathed Pies in the Milanese Style Stuffed and Empty
     5B   To Make Ten Platters of Stuffed Bagels
     5C   To Make Ten Platters of Tarts or Ten Pies
     7A   German Pastry Made For Different Means and Cowls of Saint Jacob, or Crosses; Different Animals, Fried, Fastened, or Filled With Marzipan or Cheese Filling, or Heavy Custard Sauce or Other Mixtures, To Make Ten Platters
     7C   To Make Ten Platters of Royal Pastry Stars Filled With Royal Stuffing
     7D   To Make Ten Platters of Rich Small Stars (of Pastry)
     8C   To Make Ten Platters of Stuffed Pastry of Another Kind
     9E   To Make Ten Large Pastry Shells of Eggs and Cheese

- 10A To Make Stuffed Fritters or Pies With a Filling in the German Style, Gilded
- 12A To Make Ten Platters of Macaroni in the Neapolitan Style
- 12B To Make Ten Platters of Macaroni in the Roman Style
- 13B To Make a Common Empty Pie, or of Pheasant, or Capon, or Partridge, or Dove, or Duck, or Meat of Veal, or Wether (Castrated Sheep), or Young Cow, or Venison
- 13C Pie in the German Manner With Which It Will Serve For a Day of Meat and For Lent
- 14B Pie of Pear or Apple Pieces, or in the Platters Without Pie Shells, To Vary For the Day of Meat and For Lent
- 14C Pies of Cherries or Peaches, or Plums, or Apricots, or Pears, or Apples
- 18A Pastry in the German Style of Round Fritters For Six Platters

Chapter 2 Torte DI Varie, E Diversi Sorti   87
(Pies of Various and Different Kinds)
- 19B To First Make the Ordinary Pastry For Every Pie of Two Shells.
- 20D To Make a Pie in the German Style
- 22C Pie of Morello Cherries, or Red Cherries, or Mulberries, or Melons, or Figs
- 22D Pie of Medlars, or Peaches, or Pears, or Apples, or Chestnuts, or Acorns, or Water Chestnuts, or Quinces, or of Others
- 23B Restored Pie of Flesh of Capon or of Meat of Veal
- 23D To Make a Pie of Fresh Gourds or Mulberries, or Sour Cherries

Chapter 3 Paste Per Di Di Quaresima, Gran Vigilie, Delle Qualianche Se Ne Puote Servire Per Tramezi Ne Gli Altri Giorni
(Pastry for the Day of Lent and Grand Vigil, of These You can Serve for the Middle (of Feast) and for Other Days)   110
- 25D To Make Ten Platters of Small Fritters, of Marzipan, or Ten Small Pies
- 27B To Make Ten Platters of Lenten Dainty Chewets

Chapter 4 Minestre, Da Grasso, E Magro
(Pottages for a Day of Meat and for Lent)   119

- 37C French Custard Sauce For Filling Fleur-De-Lis, Sacred Cowls of St. Jacob's Fritters and Cases For Pies, For Soup and Others
- 39E To Make Crushed Chickpeas With Pork Rind

Chapter 5 Minestre Pre Di Di Quarsima O Gran Vigilie, Magre in Tutto (Pottages for the Day of Lent or Grand Vigil, All Lenten) 125
- 42A To Make Lentils in Sauce
- 42D To Make a Pottage of Muscat Grapes, or Plums, or Figs, or Dried Morello Cherries

Chapter 6 Sapori, Diversi Si Da Grasso Come Da Magro (Sauces Diverse as Well for a Day of Meat as Well for Lent) 131
- 42F Mustard
- 45A Sweet and Strong Green Sauce
- 45E White, Black, Green and Yellow Garlic Sauce

Chapter 7 Potacci, Brodi, E Robba in Tiella, & Pignata Stuffata, in Forno (Pottages, Broths, and Things in the Pan and in the Terra Cotta Stew Pan and in the Oven) 138
- 50B Capons or Pheasants in Pottage or Others With the Broth Underneath
- 50C Pheasant or Capon or Pigeon or Breast of Veal or Other Meats Stewed in the Terra Cotta Pot in the Oven
- 50E Pheasants, or Capons, or Pigeons, or Breast of Veal, or Others Cooked in Sweet White Wine, or Vernaccia (This is Now a Kind of Dry, White Wine), or Malmsey, in the German Style.
- 51A Brain of Veal, or Capon, or Breast of Veal Underneath (A Sauce), or Others
- 52A To Make Capons, or Pheasants, or Young Fowl, or Pigeons in Savoy Cabbages, or Turnips, or Lettuces, or Onions

Chapter 8 Robbe Per Antipasti, O Tramezi, Come Polpette, Cervellti, Salciccie, Dobbe, & Altre Simili, Come Disotto Appare (Things for the Beginning of the Feast, or Middle of the Feast, Like Meat Rolls (or Meatballs), Brain Sausages, Sausages, Pickled Meat in Sauce, and Similar Others, That Appear Below) 152
- 54C Sausages On the Spit

56F Loin of Beef in the German Style

Chapter 9   Gelatie Diverse   159
          (Diverse Gelatins)
57E To Make Egg White Gelatin in the French Manner For Ten Platters

Chapter 10 A Fare Salami   163
          (To Make Preserved Meats)
59C Sausages
59E To Make Prosciutto (Italian Ham)

Chapter 11 Trattati Di Pesce   169
          (Treatises on Fish)
60C Fresh and Salted Mushrooms in Varies Ways
66D To Make Pea Pods For a Day of Meat and Lent
67A Stressed Turnips, For Ten Platters
68D To Make Onions in the Frying Pan
68E To Make Fried Gourds
68F To Make Fresh Beans in the Pod

Chapter 12 Latticini   185
          (Milk Products)
70B To Make a Compote of Rind of Melons, or Rind of Gourds, or Turnips, or Whole Unripe Peaches, By Preserving For Lent

Forward

I belong to the Society of Creative Anachronism, where we study everything Medieval and Renaissance. The period we study spans history from early cultures to 1600. My area of research in the society is period cooking, specifically Italian renaissance. In the society, we have Arts & Science events where people enter projects, including cooking, to be judged on how well we create an object or a cooking entry that would be acceptable to people from the past. Arts & Sciences also include many disciplines such as dance, performances, sewing, leather or metal work or anything they did in the past I wrote this book to help people in the SCA recreate these period recipes for feasts or entries for A&S competitions, but I also want to show non-SCA people how it was done in Italian renaissance cooking, for those who are interested. I can make myself the best Italian renaissance cook in the 21st century, but I can never be anywhere as good as the master cooks of the 16th century.

Introduction

This is a cookbook that features 51 redacted recipes from the Italian 1549 *Banchetti* by Christoforo Messisbugo. It is my understanding that this was the first book published in Ferrara Italy in 1549. The *Banchetti* has 323 recipes and the book is dived into three sections, a list of food and equipment and personnel needed to run the kitchen, a list of 13 menus, and the recipe section. I've included just a small part of what he wrote in the first section with regards to tables, lighting, breads, flours, wines, vinegars, meats, fowl, sausages, ham, lard, fresh and salted fish, oysters, chesses, fresh and salted mushrooms, butter, olives, fresh and dried fruit, fresh and dried nuts, salads, herbs, vegetables, gourds of various kinds, fennel, fresh and in vinegar, peas, beans, lemons and other citrus, rice, farrow, oil for the kitchen and for lighting and a detailed listing of all the officials needed to run the kitchen and the household. You can see from this how much it took to run a large household in the 16th century. After 1549, the *Banchetti* was taken by the Venetians and republished as the *Libro Novo*, which was published several times all the way to 1623 and must have been a very popular cookbook to have been published for that long of time.

Christoforo was born in 1500 and died in 1548. Not much is known about the life of Christoforo other than we know he was working from 1524 to 1548 in various positions in the kitchen and finished as a steward of the house of d'Este until his death in 1548. He must have done well very early on, as he was made count palatine in 1533 by the Holy Roman Emperor Charles V. This would have made him a minor noble, which is not bad for a man who started as a cook. At his death, he would have been a very high official under both the courts of the dukes Alfonso I and Ercole II. He is buried in the monastery of Sant'Antonio in Polesine Italy.

The *Banchetti* is dedicated to its patron, Ippolito II d'Este, who is one of the most interesting figures in 16th century Italy. He was born in 1509 and was the second son of Alphonso I d'Este and Lucrezia Borgia. His grandfather was Pope Alexander VI and his older brother was Ercole II d'Este. Since he was a second son, he pursued an ecclesiastical career and in 1538 was made a Cardinal. He became a great statesman and almost had a shot of becoming Pope several times, but when he could not make it himself, he was instrumental in electing other people he supported to the Papacy. He was, in every way you can say it, a true renaissance man. For further reading I recommend the books *The Cardinal Hat* and *Conclave 1559*, both by Mary Hollingsworth.

As I have said above, the second section of the *Banchetti* has 13 different menus from feasts that were done from 1524 to 1548. Here is an example of two of them:

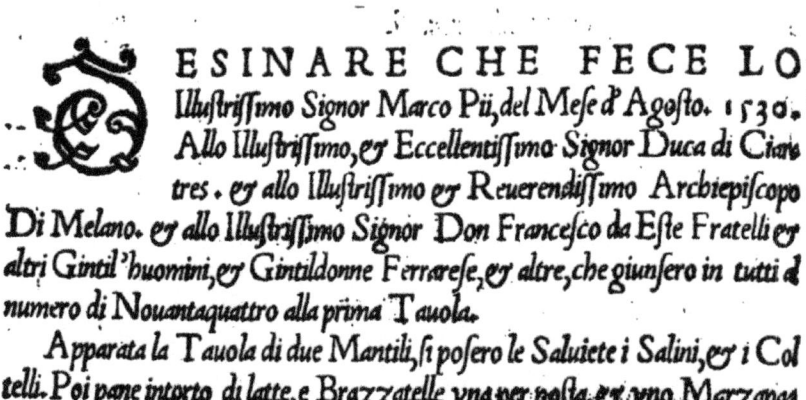

nino biscotato.
Fichi di piu sorti. in piatelli. 25.
Caui di latte vno per persona. in piatelli. 25.
Melloni. 125. in piati. 25. in piatelli. 25.
Marzolini. 50. e Formaggio parmegiano accompagnato. in piatelli. 25.
  Poi si diede Acqua odorifera alle mani, et venne la Prima Viuanda tale.
Di Coradelle d'Agnello, e Capretto piene alla Francese, arrosto. piatelli 25.
Figatelli di Polastri, Pauari, et Anarazzi, e coglioncini, e Creste e latticini di
 Vitello, e. 100. fette di persutto fritte, con Zuccharo, e Canella sopra ac‑
 compagnate. in piatelli. 25.
Polastri in bassetta. 50. e Pipioni casalenghi. 50. accompagnati. in piatelli. 25.
Pizze sfogliate. 25. in piatelli. 25.
Di Petti di Vitello, pezzi. 25. in bruodo giallo, con pezzi. 25. di Persutto, e
 fette di pan sotto. in piatelli. 25.
Polastri arrosto. 50. per migonzelli. 50. accompagnati. in piatelli. 25.
Di Carabatia di Zucche. piatelli. 25.

Pastelli piccioli. 100. di Cibibo, Datteri, et Vua passa. in piatelli. 25.
Naranzi, et Limoni.
   Nella Seconda Viuanda furono.
Conigli. 50. Polpette. 200. accompagnati. in piatelli. 25.
Di Vitello in pezzi, cioe Petti allessi coperti di sapor biaco, e fiori. piatelli. 25.
Anarazzi arrosto. 50. coperti di brognata, et pignuoli mondi sopra. in piatel‑
 li. 25.
Pastelli sfogliati. 25. di Pipioni grandetti. in piatelli. 25.
Minestra biancha di puuina di butiero passata, e Zuccharo fino e acqua rosa. in
 piatelli. 25.
Pauaretti. 25. nella Tiella. in piatelli. 25.

Nella Terza.

Spalle di Vitello, & Castrone. 25. imbroçiate, con Reti, & Osmarino sopra. in piatelli. 25.

Casatelle. 200. di frumento.	in piatelli.	25.
Pipioni. 100. nelle Zucche, con. 25. Zambudelli in pezzi.	in piatelli.	25.
Pastelli di Pere, e brogne. 25. grandi accompagnati.	in piatelli.	25.
Di Suppe dorate.	piatelli.	25.
Polpette. 200. in sapore.	in piatelli.	25.

Nella Quarta Viuanda erano.

Capponi. 25. arrosto con Limoni tagliati sopra.	in piatelli.	25.
Di Lonza Cauezzi. 25.	in piatelli.	25.
Pauoni. 25. tra grandi, e piccioli.	in piatelli.	25.
Tortelle. 25. di Ruuia.	in piatelli.	25.
Di Guanti.	piatelli.	25.
Di Gelatia chiara.	piatelli.	25.

Poi venne la Quinta Viuanda, cioe.

Ostreghe. 500.	in piatelli.	50.
Naranzi, e Peuere.	in piatelli.	25.
Giuncate. 25. grandi nell'herba con Anesi.	in piatelli.	25.
Lattemele.	in piatelli.	50.

Di Zaldoni.	piatelli.	50.
Di Persiche di piu sorte.	piatelli.	25.
Di Pere, e Finochetti.	piatelli.	25.
Carchioffole. 100.	in piatelli.	25.

E Quiui si leuò uno Mantile, & ogni altra cosa di Tauola, & si diede aqua odorifera alle mani, poi vennero le Confettioni, Tra lequali erano.

Di Confettioni siroppate.	piatelli.	25.
Confettioni bianche.	piatelli.	25.
Di Marene in Zuccharo, mastellette. 50.	in piatelli.	25.
Saluiette, bianche e Coltelli.	in piatelli.	25.
Stechi profumati.	in piatelli.	25.

LIBRO NOVO MENU IN THE MIDDLE OF AUGUST 1530

Dinner made for the Most Excellent Lord Marco Pli in the middle of August 1530. For the Most Excellent and Most Notable Lord Duke of Ciartres and for the Most Excellent and Most Reverend Archbishop of Milan and for the Most Excellent Lord Don Francesco d'Este, brothers, and other gentlemen and gentlewomen of Ferrara, and others, that arrive at in total number to 94 at the first table.

Displayed on the table with two tablecloths sat the napkins, the salt cellars, and knives, with twisted bread of milk, and a bagel per place, and a marzipan biscotti.

Figs of many kinds	In 25 small platters
Films of cream, one per person	In 25 small platters
125 Melons	In 25 small platters
50 Fresh March cheeses and Parmesan, accompanying	In 25 small platters

Then they are given sweet-smelling water for the hands, and first food arrived of this kind:

Giblets of lamb and kid, stuffed in the French manner, roasted	In 25 small platters
Livers of pullets, goslings, young ducks and testicles, crests, and veal sweet breads and 100 slices of fried Prosciutto ham with sugar and cinnamon over, accompanying	In 25 small platters
50 fried marinated pullets and 50 domesticated doves, accompanying	In 25 small platters
25 Fried puff pastries	In 25 small platters
25 Pieces of veal breast in golden broth with 25 pieces of Prosciutto ham and slices of bread underneath	In 25 small platters
50 roasted pullets, 50 young partridges, accompanying	In 25 small platters
Spanish stew of gourds	In 25 small platters
100 Small pies of large sweet grapes, dates, and raisins	In 25 small platters

Oranges and lemons

In the second food were:

50 Rabbits, 200 stuffed veal rolls, accompanying	In 25 small platters

Pieces of veal, to wit: boiled breast covered with white sauce and flowers	In 25 small platters
30 Roasted young ducks covered with plum sauce, and over it peeled pine nuts	In 25 small platters
25 Pies of coves in the grand manner	In 25 small platters
White pottage of ricotta and sieved butter; Fine ground sugar and rose water	In 25 small platters
25 Plovers from the frying pan	In 25 small platters

In the third:

Shoulders of veal and 25 wethers broached upon spits with caul fat and rosemary	In 25 small platters
200 Wheat pastries	In 25 small platters
100 Doves in gourds with 25 sausages in pieces	In 25 small platters
25 Pies of pears and plums, large, accompanying	In 25 small platters
Gilded sops	In 25 small platters
200 Veal meat rolls in sauce	In 25 small platters

In the fourth food were:

25 Roasted capons with sliced lemons over it	In 25 small platters
25 Loins of meat clippings	In 25 small platters
25 Peacocks between large and small	In 25 small platters
25 Pies of field peas	In 25 small platters
Pastries in the shape of gloves (or cloaks)	In 25 small platters
White gelatin	In 25 small platters

Then arrived the fifth food, to wit:

1500 Oysters	In 50 small platters
Oranges and pepper	In 25 small platters
Large beautiful displays of rushes with fresh cheeses and anise	In 25 small platters
Clotted cream	In 50 small platters
Rolled sweet wafers	50 small platters
Peaches of many kinds	In 25 small platters
Pears on a bed of flax	In 25 small platters

100 Artichokes   In 25 small platters

And therein is removed one tablecloth and everything on the table, and they are given sweet-smelling water for the hands. Then arrived the confections. Among these were:

Confections in syrup   25 small platters

White confections   In 25 small platters

50 Small bowls of cherries in syrup   In 25 small platters

White napkins and knives   In 25 small platters

Sweet-smelling toothpicks   In 25 small platters

ESINARE CHE FECE IL Magnifico Cōte Bonifatio biuilacqua, a lanzagallo di Sabbato alli. 8. di Settembre. 1531. il giorno della Natiuita della Gloriosa Vergine. Allo Illustrissimo et Eccellentissimo. Signor Duca di Ciartres et all'Illustrissima Sua Consorte, et al Reuerendissimo Archiepiscopo di Melano, e a Monsignore di San Benedetto, Imbasciatore del Re Christianissimo, et al Conte Hannibale di Nuuolara, et al Conte Claudio Rangone, e altri Gintil'huomini, et Gintildonne, che alla prima Tauola, furono al numero di. 74. oltre iquali si diede la prouisione per la Illustrissima Madama, e sua Famiglia, allaquale si fece la cusina da sua posta, e doppo il disinare andarono oltre po, ad vna Cazza di Cengiali, a Marara, (Anchora che esso Conte non hauesse hauuto tempo di poter mandare per Trutte, e Carpioni, et altri pesci, a i Laghi.)

Apparata la Tauola con Due mantili, Saluiette, Coltelli, e Salini, fu posto sopra essa.

Pan'intorto, vno per persona, et vna Bracciatella.
Marzapanino picciooi biscotato, vno per persona.
Di Fichi.   piati.   20.
Meggiette accarpionate con foglie di Lauro sotto, e sopra numero. 60. in
    piati. 20.
Pastelli d'Anguille. 20.   piati.   20.
Pastelletti. 80. sfogliati piccioli pieni di farro, alla Turchesca. in piati.   20.
Puuine di butiero. 40. nelle puuinarole. con Zuccharo fino sopro. in piati. 20.
Voua piene schiappate. 100. con sapore sopra.   in piati.   20.

Quando si diede Acqua odorifera alle mani, e venne la
Prima Viuanda, cioe.

Tartarette. 20. alla Italiana.   in piati.   20.
Orate. 80. fritte con Naranzi. 40. spacate sopra i piati. in piati.   20.
Di Meggie in brodetto alla Comachiese.   piati.   20.
Code di Luzzo grandi in dobba fritte. numero. 20. con Limoni tagliati, peue
    re, e aceto sopra.   in piati.   20.

Ritortéli alla Melanese grandi pieni numero. 20.	in piati.	20.
Di Maccheroni alla Napoletana cotti nel latte, con butiro, et Canella Zuccharo e formagio sopra.	piati.	20.
Suppe di brogne fresche. 20.	in piati.	20.
Gambari grossi. 400.	in piati.	20.

Poi seguito la Seconda Viuanda, et furono portati.

Rombi. 20. Passare. 40. fritte, coperte di sapore giallo Imperiale.	in piati.	20.
Pastatelle d'Vua passa, Datteri, e Pignuoli. 120.	in piati.	20.
Luzzi. 20. pieni arrosto nello spiedo con sapore di sabba, e Aceto e prasomeli sopra.	in piati.	20.
Di Tortelli alla Lambarda.	piati.	20.
Di Carabazzata di Meloni.	in piati.	20.
Di Raine grosse allesse, pezzi. 40. coperti di sapore bianco.	in piati.	20.
Di Pere guaste.	piati.	20.
Ceuali aperti misalti fritti caldi numero. 80.	in piati.	20.

Doppo laquale venne la Terza Viuanda, in cui erano.

Tortelle. 20. di Fasoli.	in piati.	20.
Frittadi di Cauiaro. 20.	in piati.	20.
Di Guanti.	piati.	20.
Di Minestra di Luzzo.	piati.	20.
Di Tomaselle da pesce.	in piati.	20.
Di Gelatia chiara.	piati.	20.
Pastelli. 20. d'Ostreghe.	in piati.	20.
Di Vermicelli di butiero lauato d'acqua rosata, et Zuccharo.	piati.	20.
Di lattemele.	piati.	74.
Di Neuole, e Zaldoni.	piati.	74.

Poi giunsero le Frutte, cioe.

D'Vua di piu sorti.	piati	20.
Di Persiche.	piati.	20.
Di Pere.	piati.	20.
Di Formaggio.	piati.	20.

```
D'Oliue.                                                          piati.    20.
Di Mandole, e Pignuoli mondi lauati in Acqua rosata.   piati.    20.
Di Codogne in quarto cotte in pignata con vino dolce, Zucchero e Canella
   sopra. piati. 20.
Di Stechi profumati.                                              piati.    20.
   E Quiui si leuo vno Mantile, et ogni altra cosa di Tauola, e si diede Ac=
qua odorifera alle mani, et poi furono portate le Confettioni, tra lequali erano.
Di Confetti stroppati di varie sorti. lib. 15.                 in piati.    20.
Mestellette di Marene. 20. Mastellette di brogne. 20. di Gelatia di Codo=
   gnata, Mastellette. 20.                                     in piati.    20.
Coltelli, e Saluiette.                                         in piati.    20.
   E Quiui fu fatta vna Musica di Voci, e Stromenti.
```

DINNER ON THE EIGHTH OF SEPTEMBER 1531

Dinner made for the magnificent Count Bonifacio Bevilacqua a Lanzagallo, for Sabbath on the eighth of September 1531, the day of the Glorious Virgin, to the most illustrious and moreover Mover Excellent Lord Duke of Chartres and moreover to the Most Lord of San Benedetto, ambassador of the Most Christian King, and to the Count Annibale of Nuvolare, and to the Count Claudio Rangone, and other gentlemen and gentlewomen that to the first table shall be to the number of 74. Much like as well was given the provisions for the Illustrious Madame, and her family, to the like is made the kitchen for her place, and after the dinner they went beyond the Po to a hunting of wild boar, to (sail?) a light pinnace (or hulk, or hoy), (although that Count did not have the time to be able to send for trout, and carp, and other fish from the lake).

Covering the table with two tablecloths, they placed the napkins, knives, and salt cellars. Things stationed were:

Twisted bread one per person, beside a bagel

Small marzipan biscuit, one per person

Of figs	20 platters
Small soused sea fish with leaves of laurel bottom and top, numbering sixty	In 20 platters
Small pies of eel, twenty	In 20 platters
Eighty puff pastry pies, small, stuffed with wheat, in the Turkish style	In 20 platters
Forty ricottas of butter in the cream dishes with fine (ground) sugar over	In 20 platters
Stuffed eggs split open with sauce over	In 20 platters
Eighty fried guilt-head (fish) with forty bitter oranges split over the platters	In 20 platters
Of sea fish in broth in the style of the Comachiese (?)	20 platters
Large tail of pike in pickle, fried, numbering twenty, with cut lemons, pepper, and vinegar	In 20 platters

Pastry wreaths in the style of Milan, large and stuffed numbering twenty	In 20 platters
Of macaroni in the Neapolitan style cooked in milk with butter, cinnamon, sugar, and cheese over	In 20 platters
Soup of twenty fresh plums	In 20 platters
Four hundred large prawns	In 20 platters

Then followed the second food and they are brought:

Twenty turbot fish, forty flounders, fried, covered with imperial yellow sauce	In 20 platters
One hundred and twenty small pastries of raisins, dates, and pine nuts	In 20 platters
Twenty stuff pike roasted on the spit with sauce of wine must and vinegar and parsley over	In 20 platters
Of pies in the style of Lombardy	20 platters
Of Spanish pottage of melons	20 platters
Of forty large boiled pieces of carp covered with white sauce	In 20 platters
Of besotted pears	20 platters

Mullet fish half-opened, fried, hot, numbering eighty	In 20 platters

After the like began the third food, in which they were:

Twenty small pies of black-eyed peas	In 20 platters
Twenty omelets of caviar	In 20 platters
Of pastry cloaks	20 platters
Of pottage of pike	20 platters
Of sausage of fish	20 platters
Of white gelatin	20 platters
Twenty small pies of oysters	In 20 platters
Of little worms of butter washed in rose water and sugar	20 platters
Of clotted cream	74 platters
Of whipped cream and spiral wafers	74 platters

Then arrived the fruit, to wit:

Grapes of many kinds	20 platters
Of peaches	20 platters

Of pears	20 platters
Of cheese	20 platters
Of olives	20 platters
Of almonds and pine nuts washed in rose water	20 platters
Of quinces in quarters, cooked in a terra cotta pot with sweet wind, sugar and cinnamon over	20 platters
Of perfumed toothpicks	20 platters

And there they removed a tablecloth and everything on the table, and they gave scented water for the hands, and then they were carrying the confections, amongst like they were:

Of comfits in syrup of various kinds, fifteen pounds	In 20 platters
Twenty marmalade tubs of cherries, twenty marmalade tubs of plums, gelatin of marmalade of quinces, twenty marmalade tubs	In 20 platters
Knives and napkins	20 platters

And there was made a playing of music and singing

The first feast had 94 at high table and the second feast had 74 at high table. The huge amount of food served in both feasts implies that other people were being served, just not at high table. Any food left over would have been used to feed the household servants and staff, or some of it might be given to the poor of Ferrara, but I can guarantee that they did not waste food. If you were eating at high table, you must have had to eat very small portions of select dishes in order to get through these feasts. The other consideration was what kind of kitchen staff would be needed to put on feasts like this. My guess it would take hundreds of kitchen workers and dozens of servers. They would have had a good supply of foods that could be done ahead of time, but look at all the pies and meats that would have been prepared the day of—a remarkable effort from the kitchens and servers. Looks like great fun to me!

Ingredients for Cooking Italian Renaissance

1. **True cinnamon (Cinnamomium zeylanicum)**
   Best place to get this is a Mexican grocery under Canella

2. **Sour grape juice**
   Best place to find this is a Persian grocery store or online

3. **Sour orange juice**
   Best place to find this is a Mexican grocery under Naranja agria

4. **Rose water and Orange flower water**
   Best place to get this is a Persian or Indian grocery

5. **Gourds (Lagenaria siceraria)**
   Best place is a Chinese or Asian grocery under Opo gourd, or you will have to grow them yourself

6. **Capons**
   Good butcher shop should have these or they can order them for you

7. **Isinglass**
   Powdered fish bladders can be found at NY Spice Shop or other places online

Italian weights and measures from the Middle Ages to the Nineteenth Century

Adapted from Ronald Edward Zupko US ISSN 0065-9738

Tables of weights and measures used in the Banchetti / Libro Novo in Ferrara and Modena, Italy

WEIGHTS

LIBRA	The Pound of the Banchetti	12 ounces	345 grams
ONCIA	The Ounce of the Banchetti		28.8 grams
PESO	The Peso of the Banchetti		19.01 US Pounds (my best guess)
DRAMMA	Dram		3.59 grams
SCROPULO	Scruple		1.198 grams
GRANO	Grain		0.045 grams

FLUID MEASURES

FIASCHI	Flask, standard at Modena is 2.083 Liters
BOCCALE	The Banchetti Bottle, Vase, or Jug is 1.385 Liters
ENGHISTARE	Carafe, standard at Verons, 0.979 Liters
BICCHIERI	The Banchetti wine glass, 4 ounces (my best guess)

DRY MEASURES

SCUTELLA	The Banchetti shallow platter	0.486 Liters 2 scant US cups

Note: The measurements above are used as a reference when recreating the recipes in the Banchetti / Libro Novo. Zupko collated measurements from many cities in Italy. The measurements presented here are selections that appear in Messisbugo's work, or are related to Ferrara or Modena (another d'Este city).

Chapter 1

Compositone Della Piu Importanti Vivande (Composition of the Most Important Foods)

1A TO FIRST MAKE FIFTY BREADS OF MILK AND SUGAR OF NINE OUNCES EACH

The first recipe is the Bread of Milk and Sugar and, as the staff of life, it deserves to be first. It is an amazing recipe because there are so few bread recipes in medieval and renaissance cookbooks, as the authors assumed you knew how to make bread. It would pass as a modern recipe except for the slight taste of the rosewater, but even with it, it is still very good, rich, refined bread. I love the fact that Christoforo gives you several shapes to make the bread and the twisted shape is the first reference of any sort to the famous couple bread of modern Ferrara.

PRIMA PER FARE CINQVAN- TA PANI DI LATTE E
Zuccharo di Oncie no-
ue L'uno.

FATTO Che hauerai la tua Sconza, o leuaturo, pigliarai di fiore di farina buratata libre. 3 5. e tanto meno quanto me
no sara quella di che hauerai fatto il leuaturo, e libre. 6. di Zuc
charo ben bianco, e Torli d'Voua. 75. e libre. 3. d'Acqua ro
sata, e libre. 6. di Latte fresco, e oncie. 6. di butiero fresco, e im-
pasterai il tuo Pane, e auuertirai bene, che l'acqua, o latte non scottasse, e farai anchora che i Torli d'Voua sian caldetti, & li scalderai, ponendoli nell'acqua calda e li porrai il coueniente sale, e farai la pasta, si che nõ sia ne dura, ne tenera, ma
piu tosto ch'habia del saldetto, e la gramarai molto bene, e poi farai il tuo pane, e lo
lasciarai ben leuare, e lo cuocerai con grande ordine, si che non pigli troppo fuoco,
ma che al tuo Giuditio stia bene, e questo pane, e piu bello a farlo tondo, che in tor
to, o in pinzoni, sia dopoi piu grande, o piu picciolo, come tu vorrai: ti gouernerai
adunque secondo questo modo, che e prouato.

When you have made your sourdough or yeast, you shall take thirty-five pounds of the flour (i.e. the finest ground) of sifted wheat and a much less amount, so that it shall be enough to have made the yeast (starter), and six pounds of good white sugar, and seventy-five egg yolks, three pounds of rose water, and six pounds of fresh milk, and six ounces of fresh butter, and you shall knead your bread. You shall note well that the water or milk does not scorch, and you shall make certain that the egg yolks are to be warm, and you shall scald them, putting in the hot water. And you shall put suitable salt, and you shall make the dough, so that it is neither hard nor tender, but harder than you shall have at firm. And you shall knead it very well and then you shall make your bread, and you shall leave them to rise well, and you shall cook them with serious method so that they do not take too much fire, but that at your very good judgment. And this bread is more beautiful by making them round, that twist, or in buns. Then they can be made larger or smaller, whatever you shall want. You shall govern yourself to one according to this way, which is proven.

Bread of Milk and Sugar (1/8 recipe)

Ingredients
1. 2 Cubes of cake yeast dissolved in ½ cup of warm (85 degrees F) water with a teaspoon of recipe sugar or a scant 1/8 cup of dried yeast dissolved in ½ cup of warm (100 degrees F) with a tablespoon of recipe flour and a pinch of recipe sugar
2. 13 ½ Cups (1508g) of soft wheat flour (I used White Lily)
3. 1 ¼ Cups (259g) of sugar
4. 10 Egg yolks at room temperature
5. 2/3 Cup (130g) of rose water
6. 1 Cup plus 4 tablespoons (259g) of warm milk mixture (a cup of whole milk plus ¼ cup of heavy cream)
7. Scant tablespoon (22g) of soft butter
8. 14 Tablespoons of warm water
9. 1 ½ Teaspoons of sea salt dissolved in above rose water

Redaction:
Use whichever yeast you want, but I am going to claim the cubes of cake yeast are a more old fashioned method. Make sure the cake yeast is at room temperature and is not too old. When I made this, the dried yeast was ready to go in 10 minutes. When the yeast mixture starts to foam or

bubble, it is ready. Place liquid ingredients and egg yolks in a bowl and mix with a whisk or place in a stand mixer bowl with a baffle attachment and mix well. Make sure all ingredients are warm or at least room temperature. Stir in the sugar and butter and start adding the flour in small amounts at low speed until it gets too thick for the baffle. Switch to the dough hook and keep adding flour until the bowl is too full, then you will have to finish by hand on a pastry board. Knead the dough very well until everything is well mixed and the dough seems smooth and elastic. This dough fixed with soft flour has very low gluten content so it does not need to rest, and the recipe will give you somewhat firm bread dough. The water I gave you should be enough, but if the dough is too dry, sprinkle a small amount of water and continue or if it is too sticky add a little more flour and continue kneading. Divide the dough into nine equal potions (this will give you 9 nine ounce loaves) and place on a cookie sheet lined with baking paper. Flatten them into rounds for a round loaf or roll in a ball for a bun or you can roll them into cylinders and twist them around each other for Jewish twist bread. When you have decided on the shape, place a damp cloth over them so they won't dry out and let rise for one hour and 15 minutes or until nearly double in size. I then cut a cross on top of them with a sharp knife (Christoforo does not say to do this, but I bet he would like it) and bake in a 350 F degree oven for 30 minutes or until nice and brown on top and they make a hollow sound on the bottom when you flick your finger on it, and let them cool.

1B BAGELS OF MILK AND SUGAR

This recipe was very interesting to translate as I first translated the title word brazzatelle as the Latin word brachium which means arm. The Italian dialect of Ferrara in the 16th century uses double z's instead of double c's many times in the cookbook. Next I checked Florio's dictionary and came across a word braccialetti which means bracelets or wristbands so I wondered where this was going. The modern Italian word I found was braccialetto, which also means bracelets or bangles or wristbands. As I continued to translate the rest of the recipe, when Christoforo says to boil the pastry in hot water and then bake in the oven and the fact that this might be a bracelet or bangle, I knew then I had a period recipe for bagels. What great fun this is!

BRAZZATELLE, DI LATTE, E ZVCCHARO.

A fare. 50. Brazzatelle, di oncie. 4. l'una. Pigliarai libre. 15. di fiore di farina, d'Acqua rosa oncie. 3. di latte libre. 3. e di Zuccharo bianco libre 2. Voua, numero. 25. di buttiero, oncie. 4. e queste cose insieme grammerai molto bene. Poi farai le tue Brazzatelle, secondo l'ordine che si fanno, e le farai leuare, con gran diligenza: Et dopoi che saranno leuate, farai bogliere la tua acqua, e l getterai dentro dette Brazzatelle a cuocere, e come verrano disopra, le cauara fuori, et le porrai in'acqua frescha, e quando d'iui le leuerai le porrai a cuocere ne forno, e se li vorrai porre anesi dentro, sera buona opera.

To make fifty bagels of four ounces each you shall take fifteen pounds of best flour, three ounces of rose water, three pounds of milk, two pounds of white sugar, twenty-five eggs, four ounces of butter, and you shall knead these things together very well. Then you shall make your bagels according to the method that is done, and then you shall let rise with careful attention, and then when they are risen, you shall boil your water, and then you shall place inside the named bagels to cook, and when they come to the top you shall take them out, and then you shall put in fresh water, and when from there you shall have removed them you shall put them to cook in the oven, and if you shall want to put inside anise, it shall be a good deed.

Bagels of Milk and Sugar

Ingredients (¼ recipe)
1. ~10 1/3 Cups (1293.7g) of soft wheat flour (3 ¾ pounds) (I used White lily)
2. 1 ½ Tablespoons (21.6g) of rose water (scant ounce)
3. 1 Cup (258.7g) of whole milk (¾ pound)
4. ¾ Cup (172.5g) of sugar (6 ounces)
5. 2 Tablespoons (28.8g) of butter (ounce)
6. ½ Cup plus 2 tablespoons of water (more or less)
7. 1 Tablespoon of bruised anise seeds (optional)
8. 1 Package of cake yeast (½ ounce) Christoforo does not list this in the ingredients but implies that it is used in the recipe.

Redaction:

Proof your cake yeast in a small bowl with a couple of tablespoons of water from ingredient 6 water and a teaspoon of sugar from ingredient 4 sugar. The yeast should start bubbling in 10 or 15 minutes. Meanwhile, place the flour in a large bowl and cut butter into the flour with your fingers. Next, break eggs one at a time into the center of the flour, mixing the flour into the egg each time. Add milk, yeast mixture, sugar, rose water and anise seeds and mix well into the flour. Start adding the rest of ingredient 6 water tablespoon by tablespoon until you get tender dough that you can roll out; you may need more or less water than I used. Divide the dough into 16 equal sized balls, which should give you a four ounce bagel. Roll out each bagel into a 10 or 11 inch rope and join them together with your fingers into a circle. Place dough rings on a cookie sheet lined with parchment paper and let them rise for 30 to 45 minutes or until doubled in size. Next, heat water in a large flat pan until it simmers and place your dough rings carefully into the pan. I did six at a time. When I added them to the water they sunk to the bottom but after a short time they rose to the top. At that time I simmered them for 3 minutes then carefully flipped them over and simmered that side for an additional 3 minutes, and then removed them from the water. When all the bagels are boiled, I placed them on cookie sheets lined with parchment paper and placed them in a 400 F degree oven for 20 minutes or until golden brown.

1C TO MAKE THIRTY SIX OF THE MOST PERFECT COOKIES

A cookie recipe was not something I thought would be in the *Banchetti*, but here we are. This cookie has high sugar content and is somewhat difficult to roll out so that is why I suggest placing wax paper over it. It also has a lot of spices in it, and I have had a lot of people ask me, "What that sharp taste is, is it ginger?" They are amazed when I tell them no, that is not ginger, but two kinds of black pepper! There are other examples in the cookbook of using pepper as a spice in recipes we would consider sweets, as well. This cookie would likely be on the table with other things at the beginning of a feast.

A FARE SOSAMELI PERFETISSIMI NVMERO XXXVI.

TOGLI Libra vna di Farina biancha, e libre due di zuccaro pisto, e ben passato per lo sedazzo, & oncia vna di Cannella fina pista, e due picicotti di Peuere pisto, e tre Torli d'Voua, & vno co'l chiaro, & vno ottauo di peziere longo, & acqua rosata mescolata con vn poco di sale, & condiligenza fa la tua pasta vn poco duretta, e menala molto bene. Poi habbi la stampa, e fa quello che vuoi stampare. E ponendoli vn pocheto di Muschio seranno migliori. Poi metteli a cuocere nel forno sopra vna asse picciola.

Take a pound of white flour and two pounds of sugar pounded, and pass it well through the sieve, and a ounce of cinnamon pounded fine and two pinches of pounded pepper, and three yolks of eggs, and one with the white, and one-eighth (ounce) of long pepper, and rose water mixed with a small amount of salt, and with diligence make your pasta a little hard, and roll it out very well. Then take the stamp and make whatever that you want to stamp and putting a very small amount of musk they shall be better, then put them to cook in the oven over a small tile.

Most Perfect Cookies

Ingredients
1. 2 ¾ Cups (345g) soft wheat flour (I used White Lily)
2. 3 and 1/3 Cups (690g) sugar
3. 5 Tablespoons (28.8g) of finely ground true cinnamon
4. 2 Pinches of finely ground black pepper
5. 3 Egg yolks plus one whole egg
6. 1 ¾ Teaspoons (3.6g) of finely ground long pepper
7. 1/8 Cup of rose water with a pinch of salt
8. A few tablespoons of water

Redaction:
Mix egg yolks and egg until they are thick and form a light yellow color in a stand mixer with a baffle attachment. Slowly add sugar while beating until it is well incorporated. Next you will stir in flour, on slow speed, then cinnamon, and the two kinds of pepper. The batter is going to be very stiff and difficult to work. Next add 1/8 cup of rose water with a pinch of salt dissolved in it. Stir in and add water by tablespoons at a time and mix after each one until you get very stiff dough. I only used two tablespoons of water for the dough to form a very stiff ball around the

baffle blade. If you get too much, the dough will become slimy and will be hard to work with. If this happens, add a little more flour and try again. Roll the cookie dough into a ball the size of a walnut. You should be able to make 36 balls. Cover them with a damp towel so that they do not dry out. Take a large cookie sheet and cut baking parchment paper to fit the bottom of the sheet. This is a very necessary step if you want to get these very sticky cookies up from the pan. Place a cookie ball on the sheet and take a small piece of wax paper and place on top and take a 3 or 4 inch flat jar lid and press the cookie out and then take a small dowel or can and roll the cookie out until it is about 1/8 inch thick and around 3 to 4 inches in diameter. This is very important for these are going to be very hard cookies and they are going to be hard to chew if you make them thick. When the cookie sheet is full, you can stamp them with an emblem; I used a ceramic laurel stamper that someone had given me. Place in a 350 F degree oven and check on them every 5 minutes until they are light brown on the top. They should take around 15 minutes to cook, and they will burn in a heartbeat due to the high sugar content. It is a good idea to rotate the cookie sheets half way through the cooking time to avoid hot spots in the oven. Remove from the oven and let cool for 10 minutes and they should come off of the paper with very little trouble. When cool, store in the fridge in an air tight container or freeze them. These are most perfect indeed!

4C TO MAKE TEN WREATHED PIES IN THE MILANESE STYLE STUFFED AND EMPTY

This next recipe is an example of renaissance puff pastry use and is very interesting in the way they created it. They roll out a thin sheet of pastry dough and add butter to it and then start rolling it on the long edge until they create a wheel and then fasten the ends together and press down on it to create a wreath. Rolling it up creates the multiple layers indicative of puff pastry and flatting it creates the wreath. It took me a while in the early days of my translation and redactions to figure this out. Notice that the recipe says you can fill it and you can leave it empty so the above discussion is what you do if you do not want it filled, either way the pastry is very delicious.

A FARE DIECI RITORTELLI ALLA MFLANESE PIENI E VVOTI.

PIGLIA Libre qnattro di fiore di Farina, *et* Torli dieci d'Voua, *et* di zuccharo oncie due, *et* di Buttiero oncie sei: *et* d'acqua rosata oncie tre, e fa la tua pasta reale, menandola vn pezzo. Poi ne farai diece parti, in dieci spoglie. Poi pigliarai di zuccharo oncie otto, *et* di Canella pesta oncie due, *et* de pignuoli mondi libre due, *et* d'Vua passa lib. vna, e messederai tutte queste cose insieme: Poi ligiermente cargerai le dette spoglie di questa Compositione, vngesdole prima con lib. vna di Buttiero frescho disfatto. Poi ne farai vn Tortiglione, a guisa di zaldone ad vno, ad vno, poi li farai in rottella, ponēdoli in due Tielle onte, non potendo stare in vna , egli andarai stendendo colle mani destramente, ponendoli tra disotto, e disopra libre due, di Buttiero, e poi le porrai a cuocere, e come seran quasi cotti, li porrai sopra lib. vna e meza di zuccharo. E per variare alcune volte vn poco di Persutto minuto, o Datteri, o cibibo tagliato in pezzi, o daltro, secondo che ti parera, e se sara di Quaresima, o Vigilia, li farai colla pasta, come si fanno i Fiadoncelli magri, come ti sera mostrato, *et* ancho li potrai fare vuoti, a guisa delle sfogliatine per variare.

Take four pounds of the flour of wheat (i.e. finest ground) and ten egg yolks, and two ounces of sugar, and six ounces of butter and three ounces of rose water, and make your royal pastry mixing it a little. Then with it you shall make ten pieces with ten pastry sheets. Then you shall take eight ounces of sugar, and two ounces of fine ground cinnamon, and two pounds of shelled pine nuts, and a pound of raisins, and you shall mix all of these things together then you will lightly fill the above pastry sheets with this composition, grease it first with a pound of fresh melted butter. Then with it you shall make a pastry, in the way of the spiral shaped pastry (recipe 2A), one by one, then you shall make in a wheel, put in two greased baking pans, not able to fit in one. And you shall work them spreading carefully with the hands, putting on them, between the top and bottom, two pounds of butter. And then you shall put them to cook. When they are nearly cooked, you shall put over them one and half- pounds of sugar. And to vary, sometimes, a small amount of minced prosciutto ham, and dates or Muscat grapes cut in pieces or others, according to what you want. And if it shall be of Lent or Vigilance, you shall make the pastry like it is made in the Lenten stuffed pastries, which you will display, and also you can make them empty, in the guise of the small puff pastries (recipe 2A), to vary.

Ingredients (pastry)
1. 10 Cups (1380g) of soft wheat flour (4 pounds)
2. 10 Egg yolks
3. ¼ Cup (57.6g) of sugar (2 ounces)
4. 1 ½ Sticks (172.5g) of butter (6 ounces)
5. 6 ½ Tablespoons (86.4g) of rose water (3 ounces)
6. ~1 Cup plus 1 tablespoon of water (more or less)

Ingredients (filling)
1. 1 Cup (23.4g) of sugar (8 ounces)
2. ~12 Tablespoons (57.6g) of freshly ground true cinnamon (2 ounces)
3. 5 Cups (690g) of pine nuts (2 pounds)
4. 2 ½ Cups (345g) of raisins (1 pound)
5. 3 Sticks (345g) of soft butter (1 pound) for spreading over pastry sheets

Ingredients (baking)
1. 6 Sticks (690g) of butter (2 pounds) (a generous ½ stick per pastry)
2. 2 ¼ Cups (517.5g) of superfine sugar (1 ½ pounds) (a scant ¼ cup per pastry)

Redaction:

Take a large mixing bowl and add the soft wheat flour and, with your fingers, work the pastry ingredient butter into it. Next mix into the flour mixture your egg yolks, one by one. Add the pastry ingredient sugar and rose water and mix everything together well. Next add water in small increments until you get workable pastry dough. You may need more or less water than I used. Remember that this dough has a low gluten content so you do not have to rest it nor work it a lot. The only thing to watch out for is the dough drying out so keep any dough you are not using covered with a damp towel.

Next, make the filling by mixing filling Ingredients 1 thru 4 in a medium bowl and set your oven temperature to 350 degrees F.

Divide the pastry dough into ten equal balls and start rolling out the first one with a rolling pin, I like the long French type without handles but the American with handles works, as well. Use a large wooden pastry board if you can. Try as much as you can to roll out the pastry dough into a rectangular or square shape and try to get it 1/8 of an inch thick or close to this thickness as you can. If you get irregular edges just fold them over and keep rolling it out. Sprinkle a little extra flour on the dough and the pastry board and the rolling pin when it starts to get too sticky. When the pastry sheet is rolled out, place around 2 ½ tablespoons of the filling butter over the pastry sheet with your hands and spread it all over the pastry sheet. Next sprinkle a ¾ cup of the filling ingredients over the pastry sheet and roll it up from the edge into a tight spiral. Carefully place the rolled up pastry on a cookie sheet lined with baking parchment paper and join the ends together with your fingers. Wet your fingers a little bit and the ends should attach very easy. Next push down on the pastry wreath with your fingers and palm to spread it out a little and make it somewhat flat. You will have to repeat this procedure for the other nine pastry balls i.e. roll them into a rectangle, spread with butter then add filling ingredients and form them into a flat wreath. These are pretty big wreaths, so you can get two to a cookie sheet, at best. When the wreaths are done, place a generous ½ stick of the baking ingredient butter on top of each pastry wreath and bake for 30 to 35 minutes or until you see a light browning on the pastry. Remove from heat and add a scant ¼ cup of baking ingredient sugar on top of each wreath and bake for 5 or 10 minutes more to finish cooking them. Do not let the pastry get too brown. This garnish sugar should be a superfine sugar or just whiz regular sugar in the food processor for a few seconds. This is a very messy pastry with all that butter (Julia Child would be proud) and sugar on them. These are very rich and tasty!

5B   TO MAKE TEN PLATTERS OF STUFFED BAGELS

This next recipe is for stuffed bagels, which are very good as a Lenten dish, but note that for a meat day it is made with the addition of the flesh from an entire capon! They did things like that in the renaissance, which makes a savory dish instead of a sweet dish, as a modern person would interoperate it. In the feasts in the cookbook, this dish would be served during the early and middle parts of the feast, but not at the end.

A FARE DIECI PIATI DI CASCOSSE.

PIGLIA Di Farina biancha libre due e meza, e quattro Torli de Voua, et oncie quattro di dileguito o Buttiero, et oncie tre di Zuccharo, et oncie tre d'acqua rosa, et vn poco di Zafarano, et impastata che l'hauerai farai due spoglie grossette, poi pigliarai libra vna di mandole ambrosine monde, e libra vna d'Vua passa, e libra vna de Pignuoli mondi, e le polpe d'un buon cappone, et oncie sei di Zuccharo, et oncia vna di Canella fina pista, e pesta bene ogni cosa insieme, con vn quarto di Peuere, e Dieci Torli d'Voua, e messederai bene ogni cosa insieme, con libra meza di Buttiero accompagnato: Poi farai le dette spoglie a liste longhe vna spana, e larghe tre dita, e l'imperai del detto pastume, lasciando bene della pasta da i lati per poterli asserare. Poi le farai in guisa di brazzatelline, e le porrai in vna Tiella onta, inrosellandole, con vn Torlo d'Vouo, e vn poco di Buttiero, et Zaffarano, et acqua rosata, e poi le porroi a cuocere nel forno, o sotto il Testo, con gran destrezza, perche non creppino.

E volendole fare di giorno da pesce, lasciarai il Deleguito, e le polpe di Cappone.

Take two and a half pounds of white flour, and four yolks of eggs, and four ounces of oil or butter, and three ounces of sugar, three ounces of rose water, and a small amount of saffron, and knead what you shall have. You shall make two somewhat thick pastry sheets, then you shall take a pound of shelled sweet almonds, and a pound of raisins, and a pound of shelled pine nuts, and the flesh of a good capon, and six ounces of sugar, and an ounce of cinnamon pounded fine. And pound everything well together, with one- quarter (ounce) of pepper, and ten yolks of eggs and you shall mix everything well together accompanied with a half- pound of butter. Then you shall make named pastry sheets in a strip longer than one span (of the hand), and larger than three digits (~3 inches), and you shall fill them with the named mixture, leaving well from pastry by the sides so you can maintain them (in other words leave enough pastry by the sides so that you can wrap them up and seal them). Then you shall make them in the manner of the small bagels, and you shall put them in a greased pan, paint them with an egg yolk, and a small amount of butter, and saffron, and rose water. And then you shall put them to cook in the oven, or underneath the mobile terra-cotta oven, with great attention, so that they do not burst. And when you want to make for a day of fish, you shall leave out the oil and the flesh of capon.

Ring Shaped Pastries

Pastry Ingredients
1. ~7 Cups (862.5g) of soft wheat flour (2.5 pounds)
2. 4 Egg yolks
3. 1 Stick (115g) of butter (4 ounces)
4. 6 Tablespoons (86.4g) of sugar (3 ounces)
5. 6 Tablespoons (86.4g) of rose water (3 ounces)
6. Pinch of ground saffron
7. ~1 ¼ Cups of water (more or less)

Filling Ingredients
1. 2 Cups (345g) of skinned almonds (1 pound)
2. 2 ½ Cups (345g) of raisins (1 pound)
3. 2 2/3 Cups (345g) of pine nuts (1 pound)
4. ¾ Cup (117.5g) of sugar (1/2 pound)
5. 4 Tablespoons (28.8g) of ground true cinnamon (1 ounce)
6. 1 Tablespoon (7.2g) of ground pepper (1/4 ounce)
7. 10 Egg yolks
8. 1 ½ Sticks (117.5g) of butter (1/2 pound)

Endoring Ingredients
1. 2 Egg yolks
2. 1 Tablespoon of melted butter
3. Pinch of ground saffron
4. 1 Tablespoon of rose water

Redaction:

Cut butter into flour and add egg yolks while mixing one by one. Mix in sugar, rose water, and saffron, then add water by increments until the dough forms a ball. Knead dough for 5 minutes or so or until everything in the dough is well mixed. Roll out dough on a well-floured pastry board to the thickness of around a ¼ inch thick or a little less. Next cut a rectangle of dough 8.5 inches long and 2.5 inches wide. This is the size that Christoforo wants in his recipe, but you can make them larger or smaller, whatever tickles your fancy.

Grind all the filling ingredients in a mortar and pestle or in a food processor, but watch the oiling effect by adding a few drops of water when you are grinding the nuts. Mix all the filling ingredients very well. Take a walnut sized ball of the filling ingredients or maybe a little larger and roll it with your hands into a rope almost as long as the pastry rectangle, and place in the middle of the pastry rectangle and fasten the edges of the strip together. It will help to fasten it if you run a wet finger around the edge. Do this carefully because you don't want the pastry to burst during cooking. Shape into a ring and attach the two ends together using a little water to help them attach. Place them on a cookie sheet lined with parchment paper and prick the tops with a fork and then paint them with the mixed endoring ingredients. Bake them in a 325 degree F oven for around 20 minutes or until they turn a light golden color.

5C TO MAKE TEN PLATTERS OF TARTS OR TEN PIES

This next recipe is a wonderful renaissance cheese tart or pie. It has a nice combination of cheeses and spices and note again the use of black pepper and also note I used three pounds of ricotta cheese, which is an educated guess on my part as Christoforo says to use four fresh cheeses without giving their weight. This is a very rich tart that I think even modern tastes would approve.

AFARE DIECI PIATI DI CASATELLE OVERO DIECI Tortelle.

PIGLIA Quattro Pouine fresche, et di Formaggio grasso libra vna, e meza, et Vuoua quindici, et di Zuccharo libra meza. d'Vua passa libra meza, d'acqua rosa oncie quattro, et di Buttiero libra meza, et oncia meza di canella, et vn quarto di Peuere, et un poco di Zafarano, e componi bene ogni cosa insieme. Poi fa due spoglie, osseruando il medesimo ordine che fu seruato nelle Cascosse, et hauerai vn bussolo grande da tagliare le dette spoglie, come sono quelli da Tortelli, poi li metterai il battuto sopra, lasciandoli tanta pasta intorno, che tu le possi spicicare. Poi le metterai in una Tiella onta, e le porrai a cuocere nel forno, o sotto il Testo, e come serano quasi cotte, li porrai sopra oncie sei di zuccharo, e poi le finirai di cuocere, e volendo le potrai fare in guisa di Tortelle, con due spoglie, cioe una disotta, e una disopra, e grandi, e picciole, come uorrai.

Take four fresh ricotta cheeses, and one and a half pounds of fat cheese, and fifteen eggs, and one and a half pounds of sugar, half-pound of raisins, four ounces of rose water, and a half-pound of butter, and a half-ounce of cinnamon, and one quarter (ounce) of pepper, and a small amount of saffron, and mix everything together.

Then make two pastry sheets; observe the same method that was fixed in the ring-shaped pastry (recipe 5B). And you shall get a large round pastry cutter to cut the named sheet, like they are in those of the pies. Then you shall place the mixture over, leave enough pastry around them that you can pinch them (up to form a lip i.e. a tart shell). Then you shall place them in a greased frying pan, and you shall put them to cook in the oven or underneath the mobile terra cotta (or metal) oven, and when they are nearly cooked, you shall put over them six ounces of sugar. And then you shall finish cooking them, and if you want, you can make them in the guise of the pies, with two pastry shells, to wit: one on the bottom and one on top, either large or small, whichever you shall want.

Ingredients (pastry)
1. 7 ½ Cups (862g) of soft wheat flour (2 ½ pounds)
2. 4 Egg yolks
3. 1 Stick (115.2g) of butter (4 ounces)
4. 6 Tablespoons (86.4g) of sugar (3 ounces)
5. 6 ½ Tablespoons (86.4g) of rose water (3 ounces)
6. 1 Pinch of ground saffron
7. ~10 Tablespoons of water (more or less)
8. ¾ Cup (172.5g) of sugar for garnishing tarts (6 ounces)

Ingredients (filling)
1. 4 ¼ Cups (1035g) of whole milk ricotta cheese (3 pounds)
2. 4 Cups (517g) of shredded provolone cheese (1 1/2 pounds)
3. 15 Eggs
4. 2 ¼ Cups (517g) of sugar (1 ½ pounds)
5. 1 ¼ Cups (172g) of golden raisins (1/2 pound)
6. 9 Tablespoons (115.2g) of rose water
7. 1 ½ Sticks (172g) of melted butter (1/2 pound)
8. 3 Tablespoons (14.4g) of ground true cinnamon (1/2 ounce)
9. 1 Tablespoon (7.2g) of ground black pepper (1/4 ounce)
10. 1 Pinch of ground saffron

Redaction:

Take a large bowl and add flour to it and work in the butter with your fingers. Next add the egg yolks and work them into the flour mixture one by one. Mix in the pastry sugar, the rose water, and the saffron, next add the water a little at a time until the flour mixture forms a ball of dough; you may need more or less water than I used to form a dough ball. Take the dough ball and cut it in half (it is a good idea to cover the other half with a damp cloth) and roll it out with a rolling pin until it is around 3/8th inch thick or a little thinner. If dough gets sticky, dust it with more flour. Christoforo says the recipe makes ten tarts around four inches in diameter, but I chose to make five eight inch tarts instead. Grease the pans with butter and place a circle of baking parchment paper in the bottom. You can make them any size you want. When the first sheet of dough is rolled out take the eight inch disposable aluminum pie pan (double them up) and place over the dough and cut a circle 1 ½ inch to 2 inches wider than the pie pan. Set the greased pie pan aside and fold the circle of dough into quarters and place half-way in the pie pan and unfold it making sure the bottom and the sides of the pan are covered in dough. Christoforo says to place filling on the pastry circle and then place in a tart pan but this seems to be very hard to do without making a huge mess! Press the dough into the sides and bottom of the pan. Roll out the other dough ball and keep making tart shells. This amount of dough will make five eight inch tarts and if you want to make pies instead, as Christoforo says, double the pastry ingredients to make the tops of the pies. Next heat your oven to 350 degrees F and then take another large bowl and mix together all of the filling ingredients. Place 3 cups or so of filling into each tart shell and place the tarts on a cookie sheet lined with baking parchment paper (for easy clean-up) and bake for around 50 minutes. It is a good idea to rotate the cookie sheets half-way through the cooking time to eliminate oven hot spots. When time is up, take the tarts out of the oven and sprinkle a scant 2 ½ tablespoons of the pastry ingredient garnish sugar on each tart and return them to the oven for 10 more minutes or until a knife inserted into the middle of the tart comes out clean. Cool tarts on a rack before cutting them or removing them from the pans. We now have a savory renaissance dish!

7A GERMAN PASTRY MADE FOR DIFFERENT MEANS AND COWLS OF SAINT JACOB, OR CROSSES; DIFFERENT ANIMALS, FRIED, FASTENED, OR FILLED WITH MARIZIPAN OR CHEESE FILLING, OR HEAVY CUSTARD SAUCE OR OTHER MIXTURES, TO MAKE TEN PLATTERS

This next recipe is just wonderful for all of the different fillings you can use in the pastry crepes. This is the beginning of what we would now call a pastry cream horn or a recipe for a cone to put ice cream in. All this from nearly 500 hundred years ago! The filling called crema will be given as a recipe later in the book, which the French call crème patissiere. The main difference between the two is they did not have vanilla in the 16th century, and used rose water instead. I have given a modern method for making the shells, but if you look at the kitchen equipment in Bartolomeo Scappi's 1570 cook book the *Opera* you can see what I translated as irons. I know that these will work because I have done it.

PASTA TEDESCHA FATTA IN DIVERSE ARMI, E CAPPE DI SANTO GIACOMO, O CROCI, E

Diuersi Animali, fritte, sutte, o piene di Marzapani, o de Mariconda, o Crema, o d'altro Pastume, per far piati dieci.

PIGLIA Libre tre di farina biancha buratata, e ponla in vno Catino, o daltro vaso netto con libre tre di latte di Vacca, e libre una di Buttiero frescho, & oncie tre d'Acqua rosa, e libra vna di Zuccharo, & un poco di Zaffarano, & Voua vinti, dieci con Torli, e chiaro, e dieci con Torli soli, e componi bene ogni cosa insieme in detto vaso, che diuenga come vna colla, poi habbi libre cinque di Buttiero frescho, o di leguito in una Patella che sia ben bogliente, & habbi i ferri ben netti, e ponli a scaldare nel grasso bogliente, poi mettegli in detta colla che se gli attaccera la pasta, e poi li tornerai nella patella, e si spiccerano da i ferri, e quando non si spiccassero bene, perche la Colla fosse troppo chiara, o troppo spessa, la acconciarai al tuo giudicio, e dopoi li porrai sopra oncie sei di Zuccharo e dette paste si possono empire, dopoi che sono fritte, di Marzapane, o Gelatia, o Mariconda, o Crema, o d'altro, e seria meglio.

Take three pounds of sifted white flour and put in a basin or other clean vessel with three pounds of milk of cow, and a pound of fresh butter and three ounces of rose water and a pound of sugar and a small amount of saffron and twenty eggs, ten with yolks and ten with yolks alone and make up everything well together in above vessel, so that it becomes like a paste.

Then take five pounds of fresh butter, or lard in a frying pan that is well boiling and take the well clean irons and put to heat in the boiling oil, then place the named paste so that it (the irons) attaches the pastry and then you shall turn them in the frying pan, and they are detached from the irons, and when they do not detach well it is because the paste is too golden (or over cooked) or too thick. You will adorn as you judge, and then you shall put over them six ounces of sugar and named pastries can be filled, after which they are fried, with marzipan, or jelly, or cheese filling, or custard cream, or of others and they shall be better.

Ingredients
1.   9 Cups (1035g) of soft wheat flour (3 pounds)
2.   4 Cups (1035g) of whole milk (3 pounds)
3.   3 Sticks (345g) of melted butter (1 pound)
4.   6 Tablespoons (86.4g) of rose water (3 ounces)
5.   1 ½ Cups (345g) of sugar (1 pound)
6.   Pinch of ground saffron
7.   10 Eggs
8.   10 Egg yolks
9.   ¾ Cup (172.5g) of sugar for garnish after baking (6 ounces)

Redaction:
Place eggs and egg yolks in a large bowl or, better yet, the bowl of a stand mixer. Take a wire whip or baffle attachment and beat eggs until they are very well mixed. Next add the sugar slowly while beating and mix very well. While you continue to mix, add the melted butter, rose water, and saffron. Slowly add small amounts of the flour to the mixture and continue mixing. Let the mixer run for some time until all the flour is incorporated very well into the egg mixture and you do not see any lumps.

Christoforo says to use the irons in five pounds of butter or lard to cook the pastry, but this is very hard to do in a modern kitchen so I came up with a quicker method by using a waffle cone maker I got online from Walmart. This machine worked very well for making round waffle pastries that you can mold while they are warm. Wipe the plates off with a wet paper towel and wipe lightly with a paper towel soaked in melted butter. Plug it in and set it for maximum heat and wait for the green light to come on. If you have it on a slick surface, it is a good idea to place a towel underneath it to keep it from sliding when you raise the top. It is now ready to cook. Carefully lift up upper plate and pour a quarter cup of batter into the center of the bottom plate and carefully lower upper plate down on top of the bottom plate and press down on grey clip in front to seal it up and time it for one minute. Crepe is done when it has a few brown spots on it, but too much brown means it will break when you roll it. When the minute is up, press down on grey clip to release and carefully raise top plate up and remove the cooked crepe from the bottom with a sharp wooden stick to catch the edge. Place crepe on a plate and carefully roll the crepe around a wooden dowel or plastic tube. You may need to wear light cotton gloves for this rolling as you do have to roll them while warm, or if it cools down too much it will break in two. Lightly grease the plates with butter before each crepe is baked. It is best to cool rolled crepes on a rack instead of a pan to keep them from becoming soggy while they cool. This recipe makes around 70 to 80 rolled crepes, which can be frozen for a month and as I show in the other recipe they can be filled with the custard sauce. They are better, as Christoforo says, if you stuff them with filling and flash fry them in a little butter to brown a bit and then sprinkle with the garnish sugar, say around a half-teaspoon per crepe.

7C   TO MAKE TEN PLATTERS OF ROYAL PASTRY STARS FILLED WITH ROYAL STUFFING

This next recipe tells how to make royal pastry stars filled with a type of marzipan, and I decided to make a Lenten recipe, which leaves out the meat. If you want to try it with meat just add boiled flesh of one capon or the same amount of boiled veal. This is very rich and tasty.

A FARE DIECI PIATI DI STELLE DI PASTA REALE PIENE
Di pastume reale.

PIGLIA di Farina biancha libre due e meza, e quattro Torli d'vo ua, & oncie sei di Buttiero, e oncie tre di Zuccharo, & oncie tre d'acqua rosa, & vn poco di Zaffrano, & impastalo, e fa due spoglie, poi piglia vna libra e meza di Mandole ambrosine monde, e le polpe d'un Cappone, e non hauendo cappone tãta polpa di Vitello allesso e lib. meza di Pignuoli, e d'acqua rosata oncie tre, e meza libra di Cibibo damaschino, cauate le anime e pista ogni cosa insieme con chiari sei d'uoua, con una lib. di zuccharo, et oncia vna di Canella, et impasta ogni cosa insieme, Poi habbi le tue stampe di gesso, o di zetto, e poneli in su la stampa di sotto il battuto disopra, e poi poni l'altra stampa disopra, e tagliali la pasta d'intorno con la speronella, o con vn coltello, e le rifermarai d'intorno intorno con le mani, poi le frigerai in Buttiero, o Dileguito con destrezza, che non creppino ouero le ponerai in vna Tiella onta, e le cuocerai nel forno inrosellate.

Take two and half- pounds of white flour and four yolks of eggs, three ounces of sugar, three ounces of rose water, and a small amount of saffron, and knead, and make your pastry sheets. Then take one and a half- pounds of shelled sweet almonds and the flesh of one capon, and if you do not want capon, use as much flesh of boiled veal and a half- pound of pine nuts, and three ounces of rose water and a half- pound of raisins, removing the seeds, and grind everything together with six whites of egg, with a pound of sugar, and a ounce of cinnamon, and knead everything together.

Then take your plaster mold or metal mold, and put on the mold, underneath the named mixture, and then put the other mold on top (this implies you put a sheet of pastry over the mold then put some filling on the pastry followed by the other sheet of pastry then place the other mold on top) and cut the pastry around with the pastry cutter or with a knife, and you shall refasten them around and around with the hands.

Then you shall fry them in butter or lard with skill so that they do not crack, or you shall put them in a greased frying pan and you shall cook them in the oven until golden.

Pastry Ingredients
1. ~7 Cups (862.5g) of cake flour (2 ½ pounds)
2. 4 Egg yolks
3. 6 Tablespoons (86.4g) of sugar (3 ounces)
4. 6 Tablespoons (86.4g) of rose water (3 ounces)
5. Pinch of ground saffron
6. ~1 ¼ Cups of water (this will vary)
7. 5 US pounds of Lard for frying

Filling Ingredients
1. 3 Cups (517.5g) of peeled almonds (1 ½ pounds)
2. 1 1/3 Cups (172.5g) of pine nuts (1/2 pound)
3. 6 Tablespoons (86.4g) of rose water (3 ounces)
4. 1 ¼ Cups (172.5g) of raisins (1/2 pound)
5. 6 Egg whites
6. 1 ½ Cups (345g) of sugar (1 pound)
7. 7 Tablespoons (28.8g) of ground true cinnamon (1 ounce)(best to weigh this)

Redaction:

First to make the pastry, place the egg yolks in a bowl or use a stand mixer with the baffle attachment and mix them very well. Next add the sugar while beating in a thin stream and mix until it forms the ribbon and is a pale yellow color. Next add the rose water and the saffron and then the flour in small batches until it becomes too thick for the baffle. Switch to the dough hook and continue adding the rest of the flour with small amounts of water until the dough forms a ball. Take it out and knead the dough by hand for a short while. Note that this dough has very low gluten content so it will not become elastic and does not need to rest. When you are not using the dough it is a good idea to cover it with a damp towel to keep it from drying out.

First peel the almonds by casting them into boiling water for a minute and then drain them and cool. Skins should slip right off. Next work on the filling by grinding the almonds and pine nuts in a mortar or food processor, watching the oiling effect by adding a few drops of rose water as you grind. Next grind the raisins. Place the ground nuts in a bowl and add the raisins and the rest of the filling ingredients and mix very well together.

Roll a small portion of the dough out on a floured pastry board until it is around 1/8 inch thick. Next cut out two identical star shaped molds out of heavy cardboard of any size you want, but best not make it too big. Next place a thin rolled out pastry sheet over the bottom mold and press around the edges a little bit so you can see the mold underneath. Place a small amount of filling in the center of the pastry and place another thin rolled sheet of pastry over the filling. Next place the second star shaped mold on top and carefully cut around both molds with the rotary pasta cutter or a knife. Next fasten the edges around the pastry with your fingers, a good trick is to wet your finger a bit and run them around the edges of the star on the bottom pastry before you pinch them together. This gets easier after the first 500 pastry stars! Sealing them is important because they can burst in the cooking oil. You can now cook them in melted lard (I used a 14 inch skillet with 5 U.S. pounds of lard) at 365 degrees. Carefully place pastry star on a spatula and lower the pastry into the hot oil and wait until it rises to the surface, about one minute. Cook the pastry for one more minute and flip it over and cook for one more additional minute and it should be nice and light brown. Do not crowd the pan, do a few at a time. Remove the pastry from oil and drain. You can also cook them as Christoforo says, in a well-greased skillet in the oven, which I think is much easier. Take a cookie sheet with a parchment paper lining and grease it with butter or lard and place in a 325 degree F oven for 15 minutes or so or until light brown and done. These are very royal indeed!

7D TO MAKE TEN PLATTERS OF RICH SMALL STARS (OF PASTRY)

This recipe is very cool because you create the pastry stars by twisting the pastry dough around the filling to make a star shape. The recipe title says they are rich and Christoforo is not kidding, as they are loaded with cheese and eggs. The recipe gives you two ways of making them, so I put my pastry in the oven, which is a lot easier. If you choose to fry them in oil or butter you will have to work hard on sealing them very tight together or they will burst in the oil. I love the fact that if you fry them, add three ounces of flour to the filling mixture—Christoforo knows best!

A FARE DIECI PIATI DI STELLETTE GRASSE.

PIGLIA di formagoio grasso gratato lib. cinque, e poi pistalo nel Mortaio molto bene, e poi ponilo in uno uaso con voua vinti, e libra vna e meza di Zuccharo, et d'Vua passa libra vna, et d'Acqua rosata oncie tre, et di Butiero libra meza, et oncia meza di Canella.

Poi piglia lib. due di Farina, e quattro Torli d'voua, et di Zuccharo oncie tre di Dileguito, ouero Butiero oncie tre, et acqua rosa, e impasta ogni cosa insieme, et fatto la pasta, dopoi farai vna spoglia nó molto sottile, ne molto grossa poi andarai mettendo sopra la detta spoglia la detta compositióe, tanto quanto seria vn Torlo d'uouo, o poco piu, e voi la tagliarai d'intorno con la speronella, ouero bussolo, lasciandoli d'intorno tanta pasta, quanto e vn dito. Poi le piccicarai d'intorno asserrandogli dentro il battuto, perche vanno discoperte quasi la meta disopra, e poi le metterai in vna patella ben'onta, e le porrai a cuocere, nel forno, o sotto il Testo, e cotte che seranno, le imbandirai ne i piati ponendoli di sopra fra tutte libra meza di Zuccharo, ouero le frigerai in libre quattro di butiero, ouero Dileguito, e volendo frigere sara buono porre nel battuto oncie tre di Farina.

Take five pounds of grated rich cheese, and then grind very well in the mortar, and then put in a pan with twenty eggs, and one and half-pounds of sugar, and of raisins a pound, and three ounces of rose water, and of butter a half-pound, and a half-ounce of cinnamon.

Then take two pounds of flour, and four egg yolks, and three ounces of sugar, of oil or butter three ounces, and rose water, and knead everything together. And make the pastry after you shall make a pastry sheet neither very thin nor very thick, then you shall proceed placing over named pastry sheet the named composition, enough as would be an egg yolk or a little more, and then you shall cut around it with the pastry wheel, or round can cutter, leave around enough pastry as is one digits (~1 inch).

Then you shall pinch around enclosing inside the mixture, because they work open on the top half. And then you shall place in a well-oiled frying pan, and you shall put them to cook in the oven, or underneath the mobile terra cotta (or metal) oven, and when they are cooked, you shall ready them for the banquet in the platters putting on top between all a half-pound of sugar, or you shall fry in four pounds of butter or oil, and if you want to fry it shall be good to put in the mixture three ounces of flour.

Filling Ingredients

1. 15 Cups (1725g) of finely shredded provolone cheese (5 pounds)
2. 20 Eggs
3. 2 ¼ Cups (517.5g) of sugar (1 ½ pounds)
4. 2 ½ Cups (345g) of golden raisins (1 pound)
5. 6 ½ Tablespoons (86.4g) of rose water (3 ounces)
6. 1 ½ Sticks (172.5g) of butter (½ pound)
7. 3 ½ Tablespoons (14.4g) of finely ground true cinnamon (½ ounce)

Pastry Ingredients
1. 6 Cups (690g) of soft wheat flour (2 pounds)
2. 4 Egg yolks
3. 6 Tablespoons (86.4g) of sugar (3 ounces)
4. ¾ Stick (86.4g) of butter (3 ounces)
5. 6 ½ Tablespoons (86.4g) of rose water (3 ounces)
6. 12 Tablespoons of water (this may vary)

Garnish
1. 12 Tablespoons (172.5g) of sugar (½ pound)

Redaction:

Mix the shredded cheese with the rest of the ingredients in the filling. Make sure you mix this very well.

For the pastry, cut the butter into the flour with your finger tips or with a dough attachment on the stand mixer. Add the rest of the ingredients except the water and mix well. Add water by tablespoons until the dough forms a ball. You may have to add more or less water than I did. Knead the ball of dough on a well-floured pastry board for a few minutes until it is well- mixed and smooth. Pinch off a small piece of dough (make sure the rest of the dough is covered with a damp cloth or is inside a plastic bag) and roll out fairly thin. Christoforo says neither thick nor thin, but this dough will get thicker as it bakes because of all the eggs in it. Place a spoonful of cheese filling in the center of the dough large as or a little larger than an egg yolk, as Christoforo says, while leaving at least an inch of dough all around the filling. Gather the sides of the dough with your fingers and carefully seal and twist the dough shut on top. It will help keep the dough shut if, before you gather it, you run your finger dipped into water around the dough edge. Place pastries on a baking sheet lined with baking parchment paper that is well buttered or oiled. Place in a 350 F degree oven and bake for around 30 minutes or until lightly golden. Place sugar garnish over top of each star, say around a half-teaspoon.

8C   TO MAKE TEN PLATTERS OF STUFFED PASTRY OF ANOTHER KIND

The next recipe is very much like the above, but instead of cheese filling it has a raisin filling. I think these two recipes compliment each other very well and would be very tasty if you did both of them for a feast. Notice that this pastry uses a good amont of black pepper, which modern taste would find unusal, but I think stills makes a very tasty pastry.

A FARE DIECI PIATI DE FIADONCELLI D'ALTRA SORTE.

PRIMA Farai le spoglie, che hai fatto in quelli di morolla sopra detti, Poi piglia libre due d'Vua passa monda e lauata, e falli leuare un boglio nel vino, e se sara dolce, sera migliore. Poi piglia libra meza di Zuccharo, et oncie sei de Pignuoli mondi ben lauati, a sei Torli d'Voua, et oncia vna di Canella pista fina, e vn quarto de Peuere pisto, et oncie sei di Buttiero, Poi in farle seruarai l'ordine sopra detto, et in cuocerle in Buttiero, e poneli la mele, et Zuccharo come e detto disopra.

First you shall make pastry sheets that you have made in those of the marrow above-mentioned (recipe 8A), then you shall take two pounds of raisins seeded and washed, and make them to simmer in wine, and if it is sweet it is better. Then take a half-pound of sugar, and six ounces of shelled well washed pine nuts, and six yolks of eggs, and a ounce of fine ground cinnamon, and a quarter (ounce) of ground pepper, and six ounces of butter, then make them as you shall observe the method above mentioned, and cook them in butter, and put the honey and sugar like it named on top.

Filling Ingredients
1. 5 Cups (690) of raisins (2 pounds)
2. Generous cup of sweet wine (I used a Blue River Riesling, a Moscato would be better)
3. ¾ Cup (172.5g) of sugar (½ pound)
4. 1 ¼ Cups (172.5g) plus 1 tablespoon of pine nuts (½ pound)
5. 6 Egg yolks
6. 7 Tablespoons (28.8g) of finely ground true cinnamon (1 ounce)
7. 2 ¾ Teaspoons (7.2g) of finely ground black pepper (¼ ounce)
8. 1 ½ Sticks (172.5g) of butter (½ pound)

Pastry Ingredients
1. 7 ½ Cups (862.5g) of soft wheat flour (2 ½ pounds)
2. 4 Egg yolks
3. 6 Tablespoons (86.4g) of sugar (3 ounces)
4. 6 ½ Tablespoons (86.4g) of rose water (3 ounces)
5. Pinch of ground saffron
6. ~14 Tablespoons of water (this may vary)
7. 5 Cups of olive oil (for frying)

Garnish Ingredients
1. 1 Cup (345g) of honey (1 pound)
2. ¾ Cup (172.5g) of sugar (½ pound)

Redaction:

Add raisins to a small pot with the wine and simmer for 15 minutes, covered. When cool, add all the ingredients in the filling, and pound in a mortar and pestle or whiz in a food processor until it forms a paste.

Place the flour in a large bowl and mix in sugar and saffron, then add egg yolks one by one, mixing them in well. Then add the water and rose water by tablespoons until it will form a ball. You may use more or less water than I did. When it forms the ball, knead it on a well-floured pastry board for a little while or until very well mixed together. Keep this dough covered with a damp cloth or in a plastic bag so that it does not dry out. Christoforo says you can make these pastries large or small, but make sure they fit in your deep fat frying pan. Mine were almost too large to fit. To make the pastry, roll out a small ball of pastry and place a small amount of filling in the center, then dip your finger in water and run it around the edge of the pastry to insure that it will stick together and place another layer of rolled out dough on top and cut around it with a pastry wheel. Seal the pastry with your fingers very well or it will burst in the frying oil. Place oil in deep fat fryer and set to 375 degrees. When it is ready, add the pastry to the hot oil very carefully with the basket and fry for around four minutes or until golden. Do not overload the fryer; just do a few at a time. Drain them on a paper towel and let cool. When all are ready for the banquet, garnish them with the honey and then sprinkle the sugar over the honey.

9E TO MAKE TEN LARGE PASTRY SHELLS OF EGGS AND CHEESE

This recipe is a rich egg and cheese pastry called fiadonie in Italian and are still being made in modern Italy. Online, there are dozens of fiadni recipes which almost all are very similar to this nearly 500 year old version. This was amazing when I first checked this a few years ago. Some things just don't change that much. I shaped my pastries into ovals, but a square, round or a rectangular shape are also used. This must be an excellent recipe if it comes to us from the renaissance to modern times. Check it out for yourself.

A FARE DIECI FIADONI GRANDI D'VOVA, ET FORMAGGIO.

PIGLIA Libre quattro di Formaggio duro grattato, e Voua vinti, e libra vna di Buttiero frescho, e libra meza di Zuccharo, et oncie quattro de acqua rosa, e libra meza di Vua passa monda, et oncia meza di Peuere pisto, et incorpora bene ogni cosa insime, e fa le tue spoglie, e Fiadoni inrosellati, e cuocili come s'e detto disopra.

Take four pounds of grated hard cheese, and twenty eggs, and a pound of fresh butter, and a half- pound of sugar, and four ounces of rose water, and a half- pound of seedless raisins, and a half- ounce of ground pepper, and mix everything well together, and make your pastry sheets and endore (or paint) and cook like it says above (9D).

Ingredients (pastry shells) (½ recipe)
1. 4 ½ Cups (517.5g) of soft wheat flour (1 ½ pounds)
2. 2 Eggs
3. ½ Stick (115.2g) of butter (4 ounces)
4. 12 Tablespoons of water (more or less)

Ingredients (endoring)
1. 2 Egg yolks
2. Pinch of saffron threads
3. 1 Tablespoon of water

Ingredients (filling, ½ recipe)
1. 12 ¾ Cups (690g) of grated Romano or other hard cheese (2 pounds)
2. 10 Well beaten eggs
3. 1 ½ Sticks (172.5g) of butter (1/2 pound)
4. Scant 1/3 Cup (86.4g) of sugar (3 ounces)
5. ¼ Cup (57.6g) of rose water (2 ounces)
6. Scant 2/3 Cup (86.4g) of raisins (3 ounces)
7. 1 tablespoons plus 1 teaspoon (7.2g) of ground black pepper (1/4 ounce)

Redaction:

Place flour in a large bowl and work in the butter with your fingers. Mix in eggs one at a time into the flour and start adding water a tablespoon at a time until you get dough that forms a ball. It may take more or less water than I used. Knead pastry dough for a little while to make sure everything is well mixed.

Place all of the stuffing ingredients into a large bowl and mix very well.

Divide pastry dough into five balls and start rolling them out into oval shapes or round shapes, whichever you want to do. Make sure the dough balls that you are not using are covered with a damp cloth so that they do not dry out. You can roll each ball into a large circle and fill half of it with stuffing, leaving at least a half inch or so around the edge, and fold them over the stuffing, fastening the ends together well. You can also divide the ball in half and roll out two round circles, fill the bottom circle and then place the top circle on top and pinch the edges together well so that it does not burst in the oven. You can also use a round pastry wheel, which cuts and seals at the same time. It is also a good idea to wet your finger in water and run it around the edges of the pastry dough to help it fasten together; you want to roll them out to 1/8 thick or a little thicker. Carefully place shells on a cookie sheet lined with baking parchment paper and cut two or three slits to let out steam then place in a 325 degree F oven for 40 minutes or until the shells are lightly brown. Remove from the heat about 5 minutes before they are done and paint each shell with the endoring ingredients, and finish cooking them.

10A   TO MAKE STUFFED FRITTERS OR PIES WITH A FILLING IN THE GERMAN STYLE, GILDED

This next recipe is for very good, rich fritters or pies done in the German fashion. It gives you many ways of shaping them: fritters, stars, and pies, which makes this a very versatile recipe for you to explore. I chose to make pies, and I want to say that I have given you modern techniques to make this recipe, but if you are doing A&S work in the SCA, you need to do all the work by hand for a good entry. Notice that there is no true cinnamon in the pie filling; what are the Germans thinking?

A FARE PASTATELLE, O TORTELLE DI MIRASTO TEDESCHO Inrosellate.

PER Fare cinquanta Paſtatelle, piglia di mandole ambroſine pellate libre tre, e de Pignuoli mondi libra meza, e libra meza di Zuccharo, e piſta bene ogni coſa inſieme, come ſe voleſti fare Marzapane. Poi gli ag giũgerai di pignuoli mondi libra meza, e libra meza d'Vua paſſa monda, et otto torli d'Voua, et oncie quattro di Buttiero purgato freſcho, et vn poco d'Acqua roſa, et incorporarai bene ogni coſa inſieme. Poi farai la tua paſta cõ farina biãcha, et acqua roſata, et Torli d'Voua, et Zuccharo, et Buttiero, et vn poco di Zaffarano, Poi farai la tua ſpoglia, e pigliarai di detto paſtume tanto quanto e vna buona Fritella, e la ponerai ſopra la ſpoglia, e la taglierai con vna ſperonella intorno laſciandoli della ſpoglia tanto che la poſſi picicare, come ſi fanno le ſtellette. Poi pigliarai vna Tiella ben onta, e ge la metterai dentro, e le inroſellerai con chiari d'Voua, et zuccharo et acqua roſata, e le cuocerai medeſimamente, come ſi fa il Marzapano.

To make fifty stuffed fritters, take three pounds of skinned sweet almonds, a half-pound of shelled pine nuts, a half-pound of sugar, and grind everything well together like if you wanted to make marzipan.

Then you shall measure a half-pound of shelled pine nuts, and a half-pound of seeded raisins, and eight egg yolks, four ounces of pure fresh butter, and a small amount of rose water, and mix everything well together.

Then you shall make your pastry with white flour, and rose water, and egg yolks, and sugar, and butter, and a small amount of saffron. Then you shall make your pastry sheet and you shall put named mixture, as much as is in a good fritter, and you shall put over the (other) pastry sheet, and you shall cut around it with the pastry cutter, leaving on the pastry sheet enough that you can pinch, like it is made in the star shaped pastry (recipe 7C). Then you shall take a well-oiled pan and you shall place it inside, and you shall paint with egg white, sugar, and rose water, and you shall cook likewise as is made in the marzipan (recipe 25D).

Ingredients (pie shells from 19 B)
1. 4 and 1/3 Cups (517.4g) of soft wheat flour (1 ½ pounds)
2. 2 Egg yolks
3. ¼ Cup (57.6g) sugar (2 ounces)
4. ¼ Cup (57.6g) rose water (2 ounces)
5. ½ Stick (57.6g) of butter (2 ounces)
6. Pinch of saffron threads
7. ~11 Tablespoons of water (more or less)

Ingredients (filling)
1. 8 Cups (1035g) of almonds (3 pounds)
2. 1 ¼ Cups (172.5g) of ground pine nuts (6 ounces)
3. ¾ Cup (172.5g) of sugar (6 ounces)
4. 1 ¼ Cups (172.5g) of whole pine nuts (6 ounces)
5. Generous 1 cup (172.5g) of raisins (6 ounces)
6. 8 Egg yolks
7. 1 Stick (115.2g) of butter (4 ounces)
8. ¼ Cup (57.6g) of rose water (2 ounces)

Gilding and garnish
1. 2 Egg whites mixed with a tablespoon of sugar and a tablespoon of rose water
2. ¾ Cup (172.5g) of finely ground sugar (6 ounces)

Redaction:

Take your almonds and put them in boiling water and then when it comes back to the boil, boil for one minute and then drain and refresh them with cold water. The skins should slip off with a little pressure from your fingers. To make the filling the old way, you would chop the almonds and pound them in a mortar and pestle, but this is a lot of work and Christoforo had a lot of workers, so I recommend using a food processor. The key here is not to overload it with almonds. I have a 14 cup Cuisinart and did it in three batches. You will have to use more batches if you have a smaller one. I added a third of the almonds, a third of the pine nuts and a third of the sugar. Pulse it several times until they look like they are grinding, then start adding drops of ingredient 8 rose water, or water, to stop the oiling effect. If you do this right, it will turn into marzipan right before your eyes! When all the almonds and pine nuts are done, add in the filling ingredients 4-8 of the filling ingredients and mix very well.

In this recipe, I decided to make pies instead of fritters. First take the saffron threads and place in the rose water and let soak for 10 to 15 minutes. Take a large bowl and place the flour in it and cut in the butter with your fingers. Work in the sugar, egg yolks, and rose water with the dissolved saffron. Next, add your water a little at a time until you get it to form a ball. You can also do this in the food processor, which is very fast. Use the dough blade and add the chopped up butter then the flour and pulse it a few times until it is incorporated into the flour. Next add egg yolks, sugar, and rose water with the dissolved saffron, and pulse until mixed. Add water a little at a time, and when you have added enough the dough will form a ball, and you are done. Do not try this in the food processor with a larger amount of dough. I made four pies with the filling, but had to make another batch of dough for the fourth pie shells. I used the disposable nine inch aluminum pie pans, but you can use regular nine inch pie pans as well. I also used two pie pans per pie as they are too flimsy to use one. Butter the inside of the pie pans and turn on the oven to 350 degrees F. Roll out a small ball of the dough on a wooden pastry board using extra cake flour to keep it from sticking to the board. Try to roll out in a circle (I struggle with this!) about 1/8 inches thick or so. There is very little gluten in this dough so it will roll out nice with a little pressure on the rolling pin. When rolled out, fold the dough into quarters and place in the greased pie pan and unfold, pressing dough into the entire pie pan. If you have a break, just take extra dough and press it into the break, this dough is very forgiving to work with. Be sure to keep unused dough covered with a damp towel to keep it from drying out. When the bottom pie crust is done, add a fourth of the filling and make the top crust making sure that the edges are well sealed and looks pretty.

When all the pies are done, place pies on two aluminum trays, and cut three slits in the top of each pie to let out steam. Bake for 35 minutes at

350 degrees F, then take them out, gild with the egg wash, and cook them for 5-10 minutes more or until light brown on the edges. When done, garnish with the sugar (Christoforo does not say to do this, but I thought he just forgot, as a sugar garnish is usually done for most of the pies in the Banchetti) and they are ready to serve.

12A   TO MAKE TEN PLATTERS OF MACARONI IN THE NEAPOLITAN STYLE

Here is a recipe for macaroni that is almost 500 years old. Pasta in Italy has been around for a lot longer than that and the talk of Marco Polo bringing it to Italy from the east is just not true. This one makes a fettuccine type of flat thin ribbon pasta or Christoforo gives you the option of the tubular type discussed in the next recipe. What is very interesting is his suggestion of placing the pasta on top of fowl, what a nice presentation!

A FARE DIECI PIATI DE MAC
cheroni alla Napoletana.

PIGLIA Libre otto di fiore di Farina, e la mollena d'un pane grosso boffetto mogliato in acqua rosata, et V oua fresche quattro, et oncie quattro di Zuccharo, e bene impasta ogni cosa insieme, e fa la tua pasta, menandola bene per vn pezzo, poi ne farai spoglie piu tosto grossette che sottili, e le taglierai in liste strette e longhette, e farai che stiano alquanto fatti. Poi li cuocerai in brodo grasso bogliente, et li imbandirai ne i piatti, o sopra Capponi, o Anadre, o daltro con Zuccharo e Canella dentro e disopra, et per li giorni da pesce li cuocerai nell'acqua senza Buttiero; et con Buttiero fresco se vorrai.

Take eight pounds of 'flower of wheat' (i.e.- finest ground flour), and the crumb of a rich fine bread soaked in rose water, and four fresh eggs, and four ounces of sugar, and knead well everything together, and make your pastry, mixing it well for a little while.

Then with it you shall make pastry sheets rather quickly somewhat thick than thin, and you shall cut them in long narrow strips and you shall make like some are made (i.e.-like recipe 12B).

Then you shall cook them in good rich boiling broth, and you shall ready them for the banquet in a platter, or over capons or ducks or else others, with sugar and cinnamon inside and on top. And for a day of fish, you shall cook them in water without butter, or with fresh butter if you shall want.

Ingredients
1. 24 Cups (2760g) of soft wheat flour (eight pounds)
2. 2 Cups of Panko bread crumbs
3. ½ Cup of rose water
4. 4 Eggs
5. ½ Cup (115g) of sugar (4 ounces)
6. 2 ½ to 3 Cups of water (more or less)
7. 3 Gallons of good beef or chicken stock or just water
8. 4 Tablespoons of sugar with 3 Tablespoons of ground true cinnamon or to your taste

Redaction:
Place the bread crumbs in a bowl and add rose water and mix well. Let sit and soak for ten minutes then squeeze out excess rose water with your hands. Place eggs in a large stand mixture with a baffle attachment and mix them very well. Add your sugar in a thin stream and mix until it forms the ribbon and is a light yellow color. Next add the soaked bread crumbs and mix in very well. Switch to a dough hook on your stand mixer and add small amounts of the flour until it becomes somewhat thick, and then add some of the water to thin it out a bit. This is a large recipe so you are going to have to do it in stages. When all the flour and water is mixed

in you are aiming for somewhat stiff dough.   Take a portion of the dough and roll it out on a floured pastry board until it is somewhat thick, say a quarter inch or less and then roll it up like a tube and cut it into narrow strips. Make sure any unused dough is covered with a damp towel. Christoforo now says you also can make the pasta like it is done in the recipe 12 B with the dowel. This is now your choice which one. Cook the pasta in the boiling broth until it is al dente, which will not take long if it is fresh, it will take longer if you dry it out. When you have cooked the pasta, toss it with most of the cinnamon and sugar and place the rest on top. Christoforo says this pasta can be used on a platter or to cover capons or ducks or other fowl.

12B   TO MAKE TEN PLATTERS OF MACARONI IN THE ROMAN STYLE

This in another macaroni recipe that takes the shape of a hollow tube, which I think we all are familiar with. It certainly would be a lot of work to do it this way for a lot of pasta, but the kitchen had a lot of workers. My understanding is that macaroni was not that popular outside the rich people until the industrial revolution came up with mechanical extruding the pasta, which made it for everyone.

> A FARE DIECI PIATI DE MAC,
> cheroni Romaneschi.
> PIGLIA Libre cinque di Farina biancha, e la mollena d'un pane bof
> fetto mogliato in acqua rofata, e Voua tre, et oncie tre di Zuccharo, e fa vna pa
> fta, e dopoi falla in fpoglie piu tofto groffe che minute, et inuolgile intorno ad vn
> baftone, e poi caua fuori detto baftone, e taglia la pafta larga vn dito, et feran co
> me butelli, iquali ne i di da carne porrai a cuocere in buono brodo graffo che bo
> glia quando li gettarai a cuocere, e poi li imbandirai, ponendoli imbandendo buo
> no Formaggio duro grattato, e Zuccharo é Canella, e difotto e difopra e per
> mezo, et i giorni che non fono da carne, li potrai cuocere nell'acqua che boglia
> con Buttiero, o varamente nel latte, non lafciando mai il conueniente fale.

Take five pounds of white flour and a loaf of fine bread without crusts soaked in rosewater, and three eggs, and three ounces of sugar and make pastry dough, and then make pastry sheets a little more harder and thicker than thin and wrap around on a dowel and then remove the dowel and cut the pasta larger than a finger digit (i.e. a little over an inch long), and they are like intestines, and these on a meat day you shall put to cook in good rich broth that is boiling when you cast them to cook. And then you shall ready them for the banquet, put good hard grated cheese, and sugar and cinnamon, on the bottom and on top and in the middle. And the day that is not to be of meat, you may cook them in boiling water with butter, or truly in milk, do not ever leave out suitable salt.

Ingredients
1. 15 Cups (1725g) of soft wheat flour (5 pounds)
2. 2 Cups of Panko bread crumbs
3. ½ Cup of rose water (may need more)
4. 6 Tablespoons (86.4g) of sugar (3ounces)
5. 3 Eggs
6. 2 to 2 ¼ Cups of water (more or less)
7. 2 ½ Gallons of good stock or water
8. 2 to 3 Cups of freshly grated Parmigiano-Reggiano cheese
9. 3 Tablespoons of sugar or to your taste
10. 2 Tablespoons of finely ground true cinnamon or to your taste

Redaction:
Place the bread crumbs in a bowl and add the rose water and mix well. Let stand for ten minutes, then squeeze out excess rose water. Place flour in a large bowl and stir in the eggs and the bread mixture with the sugar. Next add water in small increments until you get stiff dough. Do not add too much water or you will not be able to get the dough off the dowel. Knead for a while until smooth and lump free. Roll out part of the dough on a pastry board until it is somewhat thin, say around 1/8 inch thick, but not too thin or again you will not be able to get the dough off of the dowel. Take a dowel, say a round chop stick, flour it well with wheat starch, and cut a strip of dough, say an inch or more wide and as long as your dowel, and wrap the dough around the dowel and pinch and fasten

it together with your fingers. It may help if you wet your fingers to get the edges of the dough to stick together. Then wiggle the dowel a bit to get it to come out from the pastry tube. If it won't come out, let sit a while for the dough to dry out a bit, then try again. It is a good idea to let the empty pastry tubes dry out a bit before you cut them. Cut them as Christoforo says, into 1 ¼ to 1 ½ inch long rounds. Another trick is to cut them while on the dowel and then let them dry a bit so that they will more easily come off the dowel. Next bring your stock or salted water to the boil in a large pot and add pasta to the pot. Wait until it comes back to the boil and cook from 1 to 5 minutes depending on how much you let the pasta dry out. If pasty is fresh it will take a very short time and when it starts to float on top of the water check for doneness. Should be soft but with a little bite (i.e. al dente) Do not overcook the pasta. When ready to serve ,take a large platter and cast cheese, cinnamon, and sugar on the bottom add half of the pasta, dust with more cheese, cinnamon, and sugar, then the rest of the pasta and garnish top with cheese, dust with sugar and then the cinnamon.

13B TO MAKE A COMMON EMPTY PIE, OR OF PHEASENT, OR CAPON, OR PARTRIDGE, OR DOVE, OR DUCK, OR MEAT OF VEAL, OR WETHER (CASTRATED SHEEP), OR YOUNG COW, OR VENISON

For the next recipe, a pork pie and all kinds of meat options to vary. This one is unusual, for Christoforo does not pre-cook the meat as far as I can tell. Notice also that he uses only one pastry sheet so I decided to enclose the pie by twisting the top of the dough to seal the top. I don't know if this is what he wanted, but is very interesting looking. You could also seal it like a pouch whatever you like. Christoforo also gives a lot of options for the sour fruit to put in the filling so it is a very versatile dish.

A FARE VNO PASTELLO, SVTTO COMMVNE, O DI FAGIANO,
o Cappone, o Pernice, o Pizzoni, o Anadre, o Carne di Vitello, o Castrone, o Manzo, o Venasone.

LO Ordinario sera questo per lo commune. Prima pigliarai libre due di Farina, Voua due, oncie quattro di Buttiero, & acqua, & impastarai la pasta che resti grossa mezo dito, e piu, poi pigliarai il Fagiano, o altro Vccello, o pezzo di carne bene inpillottato, poi pigliarai vna buona cucchiara di specie miste, & vn pochetto di Zaffrano, e lo inuolgerai atorno l'Vccello, o Carne, con qualche fetta di Limone tagliato, volendogene, e qualche ramella di finocchietto frescho, o qualche grano d'Agresto, o Marene, o il succo di due Narance, e auuertissi che s'egli sera di Porcho domestico, o saluatico, o Castrone, li potrai porre manco lardo, & cosi serrato il Pastello, lo farai cuocere nel forno.

The usual, is this for the common (or every day). First you shall take two pounds of flour, two eggs, four ounces of butter, and water, and you shall raise a large pastry sheet that remains a half-digit (thick) or more.

Then you shall take the pheasant, or other fowl, or well-rounded pieces of meat. Then you shall take a good tablespoon of ground spices, and a pinch of saffron, and you shall wrap around the fowl or meat, with some lemon slices cut just as you like, and some branches of young fresh fennel, or some grains of green grapes, or cherries, or the juice of two sour oranges. And notice when it is speaking (the recipe) of domesticated or wild pork, or weather, you can put less fat, and enclose this pie, and you shall make it to cook in the oven.

Ingredients (pastry)
1. 6 Cups plus a scant ¼ cup (690g) of soft wheat flour (2 pounds)
2. 2 Eggs
3. 1 Stick (115.2g) of butter (4 ounces)
4. ~14 Tablespoons of water

Ingredients (filling)
1. 1 ½ Cups of pork butt or loin cut into 1.5 inch chunks (make them attractive rounded ovals as Christoforo says if this is a A&S entry)
2. A tablespoon of mixed spices to wit: a teaspoon of ground true cinnamon, ¾ teaspoon of salt, ¾ teaspoon of ground black pepper, ½ teaspoon of ground ginger
3. Pinch of saffron
4. ½ Lemon peeled and cut into slices
5. 2 Tablespoons of chopped fresh fennel bulb with 3 or 4 sprigs of fennel leaves
6. 2 Tablespoon of rendered pork lard if you use pork loin

Redaction:
Place the flour in a large bowl and with your fingers work in the chopped chilled butter until it is mixed in. Next work in the eggs and start adding water to the flour ¼ cup at a time until in starts forming a ball.

Knead the dough a little bit and then cover with a damp towel if you are not ready to roll it out. This can be done quickly if you have a Kitchen aid mixer (I have a 6 quart size). Place the flour in the mixer bowl and attach the baffle blade and mix in the chilled butter on a slow speed until well mixed, then add egg yolks and mix them in. Next add water in increments until the dough starts to form a ball, and remove from the mixer and knead a bit. This dough has very low gluten content so you don't have to give it a rest, but it will dry out very quickly. When ready to roll it out, place the dough on a large pastry board and roll out a large circle that is ½ inch thick, as Christoforo says. Place pastry in a 9 inch well-greased pie pan and start adding the filling. First place the meat in and then the lemon slices (cut the lemon in ½ inch slices and then cut the rind off with a sharp knife and hold them up to the light to remove the seeds), add fennel leaves and bulb, then the saffron and spices. Enclose the pie with the dough, wetting both ends with water to get them to stick together. I tried to twist the top together to form a spiral, but it did not turn out as good as I wanted, but at any rate fasten the top together. Cut three slits in the sides to vent off steam and bake in a 325 degree F oven for 90 minutes and then turn temperature to 425 degrees F for 10 minutes to brown some more. Very interesting dish, but I think it needs a sauce such as sweet and strong green sauce (recipe 45 A) or Agliata garlic sauce (recipe 45 E).

13C   PIE IN THE GERMAN MANNER WITH WHICH IT WILL SERVE FOR A DAY OF MEAT AND FOR LENT

I now have a very interesting recipe, which for all practical purposes is a renaissance chess pie. I would have loved for Christoforo to have given measurements, but on occasion he does not. The reference to recipe 14A is also not complete, as he does not call for any eggs in the pastry and you must have eggs or egg yolks to up the protein contents or it will not work. Because the pastry has saffron in it, this turns the filling a very green color, which I am sure they liked when serving it. They liked color in their food in the renaissance!

> PASTELLO ALLA TEDESCHA DI CVI SENE SERVE DA grasso, e da magro.
>
> FARAI La casa del Pastello, o grande o picciola, secondo che tu vorrai, del medesimo modo che hai fatto quella delle frutte tonde, poi pigliarai Voua battute, et Zuccharo, et acqua rosata, in quella quantitade che al tuo giudicio parera, e secondo che sera il Pastello, e messederai bene ogni cosa insieme, e imperai la cassa, e la ponerai nel Forno a cuocere senza coperto, e come sera cotto li porrai sopra del Zuccharo.

You shall make the case for the pie, either grand or small, according to what you shall want, in the same way that has been made of those of the round fruit pies (recipe 14A). Then you shall take beaten eggs, and sugar, and rose water, in those quantities that to your judgment seems to like and according to what is the pie. You shall mix everything well together and you shall fill the case, and you shall put it in the oven to cook without a top. And when it is cooked you shall put over it the sugar.

Ingredients
Filling (for one pie bottom)
1. 5 Beaten eggs
2. 1.5 Cups (317.9g) of sugar
3. 2 Tablespoons of rose water
4. 2 Tablespoons of garnish sugar for each pie

Pastry (for two pie bottoms)
1. 5.5 Cups (517.5g) of soft wheat flour
2. 2 Egg yolks
3. ¼ Cup (57.6g) of butter
4. 1/8 Teaspoon of ground saffron
5. 15 Tablespoons of water (more or less)

Redaction:
    Add the flour to a large bowl and cut the butter in with your fingers and mix in the egg yolks and saffron. Add water to the mixture a few tablespoons at a time until you get dough that forms the ball and you can roll out. This dough has very low gluten content so weather and working it is not a problem and it does not need to rest, just keep it from drying out too much with a damp towel. When you can roll dough, divide into two equal portions, as this recipe will make two 9 inch pie crusts bottoms. Roll out between a 1/8 to ¼ inch thick circle, fold into fourths, place in a greased pie pan and unfold pressing it down on the pie pan and heat oven to 350 degrees F.

Beat the eggs together very well and slowly add your sugar and then the rose water do not over beat the filling mixture. Fill one pie bottom with filling and make another batch for the other pie bottom. Bake pies for 50 minutes (rotate pies halfway through the time in case there are hot spots in the oven) and add the garnish sugar to each pie and bake for 5 to 10 more minutes or until a knife inserted in the middle comes out clean.

14B   PIE OF PEAR OR APPLE PIECES, OR IN THE PLATTERS WITHOUT PIE SHELLS, TO VARY FOR THE DAY OF MEAT AND FOR LENT

This next recipe is a delightful pear or apple filling that can stand by itself or you can bake it into a pie. It is very fruity and spicy and also very versatile as it can be used for a meat day and a lean day. I used a heavy red sweet wine, which is just perfect with the fruit and spice, but a Moscato will work as well.

PASTELLO DI PERE GVASTE, O POME, OVERO NE I PIATEL li senza Paſtello per variare il Di da graſſo, e da magro.

PIGLIA i Peri, o Pomi in quella quantita per i Paſtelli, o Piati che vorrai fare, eʒ penſo che ſei per paſtello, e otto per piatto baſtarano a iquali darai vna buona sbraſata nel fuoco, poi li leuerai, eʒ come ſarano rafredati li mondarai laſciando in mezo il picollo, e poi che ſarano mondati li ponerai in vn vaſo a bogliere in buono Vino nero con Zuccharo aſſai, e qualche pezzo picciolo di Canella integra, e pochi Garofani integri, e laſciarai cuocere, facendo che il ſapore ſia ſpeſſetto, che parera proprio vna Gelatia, e volendoli in Paſtello, hauerai parecchiate le caſſette, e l'imperai, ouero che l'buuanurai ne i piati, e ſpargia bene ſopra qualche Canellino confetto. Penſo che a fare vno de queſti Paſtelli li andara di Zuccharo oncie ſei, eʒ di Canella meza oncia, eʒ Garofani numero, dieci, e poi ſopra i Paſtelli, o piati Aneſi, o Canellini confetti.

Take the pears or apples, in the quantity for the pies or platters that you shall want to make, and I think that six per pie, and eight per platter are enough, to which you shall give a good baking in the oven, then you shall remove them, and when they are cooled, you shall peel (and core them) leaving in half the small. And then when they are peeled you shall put them in a pot to boil with good red wine, with enough sugar and some small pieces of whole cinnamon and a small amount of whole cloves, and you shall leave to cook, make the sauce to be a little thick that appears typical of a gelatin (recipe 57D).

And if you want them in a pie, you shall have several pie cases and you shall fill them, or you shall ready for the banquet in the platter, and lie well over them well some candied cinnamon.

I think that to make one of these pies go with six ounces of sugar and a half-ounce of cinnamon, and ten cloves, then over the pies or platters anise or candied cinnamon.

Ingredients (pear filling)
1. 6 Pears
2. 1 Cup of red wine (I used Elysium desert wine)
3. ¾ Cup (172.8g) of sugar (6 ounces)
4. 1 quill of true cinnamon (14.4g) (~5 inches long and 1 inch wide)
5. 10 Cloves
6. ½ Tablespoon of anise seeds

Redaction:
First bake the pears in a flat pan in a 350 degree F oven for 15 minutes. Remove them to cool and then peel them. Cut them in half and remove the core and cut them into large pieces. Place them in a pot and add wine, sugar, quill of cinnamon and cloves. Wrap cinnamon in cheese cloth and

tie it securely, as you don't want it to come apart (trust me on this!) Simmer the mixture for around 40 minutes or until it becomes somewhat thick. You can serve it like this with anise seed over it, or you can put in a pie shell.

Use the same pastry recipe and procedure as the peach pie recipe on 14C and place the anise seed on top of the pie.

14C PIES OF CHERRIES OR PEACHES, OR PLUMS, OR APRICOTS, OR PEARS, OR APPLES

Here is another recipe in which Christoforo gives you many choices of fruit to use in the pie. I used peaches because it is one of my favorites, but all the different fruits are very good. This makes a rich, spicy pie. As in recipe 13C, Christoforo says to use 14A pastry, which I have done with the addition of egg yolks.

> PASTELLI DI MARENE, O PERSICHE, O BROGNE, O MVNIACHE, o Pere, o Pome.
>
> FARAI La Caſſa del Paſtello del modo che fu quella del Paſtello di Codogne, che ſia larghetta nel fondo, e che ſi venga ſtringendo diſopra; Poi per vn Paſtello, pigliarai libra vna di Marenne a buon peſo, monde da i picolli, e nel fondo della Caſſa del Paſtello, le diſtenderai politamente, poi li metterai oncie cinque di Zuccharo, eʒ oncia meza di buona Canella fina, eʒ oncie cinque di Buttiero freſcho, eʒ poi li farai il ſuo coperto tagliato diſopra in tre luochi, poi lo cuocerai deſtramente; E'l ſimile farai in quelli delle altre frutte. Ma auuertiſſi che le altre frutte uan pellate, e le pellerai facilmente in queſta maniera, Sboglienzandole in Vino, od acqua, eʒ poi che ſaranno raffredate pellandole, eʒ alle Pere moſchardine li laſciarai mezi i picolli.

You shall make the shell of the pie in the mode that was the same as the quince pie (recipe 14A), that is wider in the bottom and that is to be pressed on top (or over).

Then for one pie you shall take a pound of cherries to a good weight (i.e. crush), remove from the seeds, and in the bottom of the pie you shall spread neatly. Then you shall place five ounces of sugar, and a half-ounce of good fine (ground) cinnamon, and five ounces of fresh butter, and then you shall make your cover cutting on top in three places.

Then you shall cook carefully.

And you shall make in a similar fashion those of the other fruits. But notice that the other fruits you want to peel, and you shall peel them most easily in this manner, soak them in wine or water, and then when they are refreshed, peel them. And in the Italian (Muscadine pear) you shall leave in half the small ones.

Ingredients (pastry from 14A and 19B)
1. 4 and 1/3 Cups (517.5g) of soft wheat flour (1.5 pounds)
2. 2 Egg yolks
3. ½ Stick (57.6g) of butter (2 ounces)
4. 10 Tablespoons of water (more or less)
5. Pinch of saffron threads (use 4 tbs. of above water to dissolve it)
6. ¼ Cup (57.6g) of sugar (2 ounces)
7. ¼ Cup (57.6g) of rose water (2 ounces)

Ingredients (peach filling)
1. 2 Cups (345g) of sliced peaches (1 pound)
2. 2/3 Cups (144g) of sugar (5 ounces)
3. 3 ½ Tablespoons (14.4g) of ground true cinnamon (½ ounce)
4. 1 Stick plus 2 Tablespoons (144g) of butter (5 ounces)

Redaction:

First dissolve the saffron in a ¼ cup of pastry water. Place the flour in a bowl and work in the chopped butter with your fingers, then work in the egg yolks and then stir in the sugar and rose water. Add the water to the mixture by tablespoons including the saffron water. When it forms the ball, knead it for a little while to mix everything well. Cover pastry with a damp cloth to keep it from drying out. If you have a 14 cup Cuisinart you can do this pastry very fast and easy. Fit the large bowl with the pastry blade and run the machine on the pastry setting. Place flour in bowl and add chopped butter and whiz a few times to blend. Next add the egg yolks, sugar, and rosewater and whiz a few times to mix well. While running the machine, add your water a tablespoon at a time until it forms a ball. Take it out and knead it a little and you're done. Take 2/3 of the pastry and roll out as thin as you can, fold into quarters and unfold into a well-greased 9 inch pie pan. Roll out the cover with the rest of the dough for the top the pie.

Soak three peaches in cool water for an hour, as Christoforo says, and peel. Cut them in nice slices and place in an attractive manner in the dough bottom of the 9 inch pie pan. Next melt the filling butter and pour over peaches and place over the cinnamon and sugar. Take your pie top and fold into quarters and unfold on top of pie. Seal the edges well and try to make as attractive as you can. Cut the pie in three places to let steam out and bake in the middle of a 350 degree F oven for 45 minutes or until lightly brown.

18A   PASTRY IN THE GERMAN STYLE OF ROUND FRITTERS FOR SIX PLATTERS

This next recipe is very exciting, as it looks like an early recipe for *pate choux* and will make a baked shell just like Julia Childs recipe in the *Art of French Cooking* Volume 1. It is not quite as good as the modern one, but is close. I tried this and was amazed! I do not know if they tried to make a shell in the 16th century as this recipe is for fritters cooked in oil and are very good on their own. Early modern cooking indeed!

> PASTA TEDESCHA IN FRITEL-
> le tonde, per piati sei.
>
> PIGLIA Scutelle due d'acqua di po, et oncie due d'acqua rosata, cō oncie quattro di Zuccharo, et oncie quattro di Buttiero frescho, e poi metti dette robbe al fuoco in vna Cazza, e come ha leuato il boglio, piglia libre due di fióre di Farina, e gettala nella detta Cazza che boglia, e mescolala cosi un pochetta, poi leuala dal fuoco, e mettila a rafreddare, pero sempre mescolandola, fino a tanto che sera ben fredda, poi piglia detta compositione, e mettila nel mortaio, e pista la ponendoli cosi pistando Voua sei détto ad vno, ad vno, et i chiari, et i Torli insieme, et un poco di Zaffrano, e finita de porli l'Voua sempre pistandola, pia gliarai lib. tre di Dileguito, o Buttiero in vna patella che boglia, e con vna cuc- chiara li getterai dentro le Fritelle ad una ad una, e cotte volendole imbandire li porrai oncie quattro di Zuccharo sopra.

Take two platters (~four cups) of water of the Po, and two ounces of rose water with four ounces of sugar, and four ounces of fresh butter, and then put named things to the fire in a pot, and when it simmers, take two pounds of the flour of wheat (finest ground white flour) and cast it in the named pot when boiling, mixing this a little.

Then remove from the fire and put it to cool, but always stirring until it is enough that it is well cooled, then take named composition and put it in the mortar and grind. Put inside this mixture six eggs, one by one, and the whites and yolks together, and a small amount of saffron, and always grinding finish with adding the eggs, you shall take three pounds of lard, or butter in a pot that's boiling, and with a tablespoon you shall cast inside the fritters one by one, and cook, wanting to ready for the banquet you shall put over them four ounces of sugar.

Ingredients
1. 4 Cups of water
2. 5 Tablespoons (57.6g) of rose water (2 ounces)
3. ½ Cup (115.2g) of sugar (4 ounces)
4. 1 Stick (115.2g) of butter (4 ounces)
5. 5 and 2/3 Cups (690g) of soft wheat flour
6. 6 Large eggs
7. Pinch of ground saffron
8. 5 Cups (1035g) of light olive oil
9. ½ Cup (115.2g) of sugar for garnishing the fritters (4 ounces)

Redaction:
Place ingredients 1 thru 4 in a large pot and bring to the boil and carefully cast inside all of the flour while stirring with a heavy paddle or spoon. Heat the flour mixture for a couple of minutes to cook the flour. Remove from heat and let cool while stirring it every now and then. When the dough is cool, stir in the eggs one by one into the dough, making sure each egg is well mixed into the dough before adding another one and also stir in the saffron. The dough mixture is very stiff, so it is best to do what Christoforo says and use a large mortar with a pestle to mix it or a large heavy pot with a large wooden paddle or spoon. When all the eggs are added and the dough is cool or just a little warm, start heating up the olive oil to 375 degrees F in a skillet or in an electric deep frying pot. I used a

deep fryer that holds 1.7 liters (~5 cups) of light olive oil. When the oil reaches temperature, make your fritters with a tablespoon, but I found it easier to just use your hands. Roll them in balls an inch or an inch and a quarter in diameter, but not much larger as they will be hard to get done. I also used a frying basket, which helps out a lot. I got 15 in the basket, but do not put too many as you will lower your oil temperature too much. I cooked them around 15 minutes or until they turn a nice golden brown. Remove the basket from the heat and drain on paper towels and when all the fritters are done garnish with the ingredient 9 sugar.

Chapter 2

Torte DI Varie, E Diversi Sorti
(Pies of Various and Different Kinds)

19B   TO FIRST MAKE THE ORDINARY PASTRY FOR EVERY PIE OF TWO SHELLS.

This next pastry recipe is the template for almost all of the following pie recipes and others in many places in the *Banchetti*. I think it is very interesting that Christoforo gives a common and a recipe in all perfection. Looks like the second one is used for special occasions and the common is for day to day operations. Notice in this one and many like it the use of saffron to color the pastry yellow. This color was a status symbol as it was the most expensive spice in the 16th century and guess what, the most expensive spice in the 21st century is still saffron! Notice that Christoforo gives you a way to make the pies more beautiful by endoring them with egg yolk, saffron and rose water, which you can do if you want for all the pies that follow.

Prima à fare la pasta commune ad ogni Torta da due spoglie.

Prima piglia di Farina biancha libra una e meza, & Torli due d'uoua, & oncie due di Butiro, & Acqua & un goccio di Zaffrano per la commune, & quando la vorrai in tutta perfettione gli aggiungerai oncie due di Zuccaro, et oncie due d'Acqua rosata, e così la impastarai e farai le tue spoglie, o à uno modo, o à l'altro, secondo che tu vorrai spendere, & quando le torte da due spoglie seranno mezo cotte, per bellezza li potrai dare la Rosella con un Torlo d'uouo & vn poco di zaffrano, & acqua rosata, che fara bel vedere, e in quelle che seranno d'una spoglia sola pigliarai la metà delle sopradette cose.

First take a pound and a half of white flour, and two egg yolks, and two ounces of butter, and water, and a spot of saffron for the ordinary (pie), and whenever you shall want every perfection you shall measure two ounces of sugar, and two ounces of rose water, and this you shall knead and you shall make your shells, in one way or another, according to what you shall want to use.

And whenever the pies of two shells are nearly cooked, for decoration you can give it a rosy coloring with an egg yolk, and a small amount of saffron, and rose water, which shall make it beautiful to see. And in those that are one shell alone you shall take half of the above-mentioned things.

Ingredients
1. 4 ¼ + 1/8 Cups (518.2g) of soft wheat flour (1 ½ pounds)
2. 2 Egg yolks
3. Generous ¼ cup (57.6g) of butter (2 ounces)
4. 8 Tablespoons of water (more or less)
5. Small pinch of ground saffron
6. Scant 5 Tablespoons (57.6g) of sugar (2 ounces)
7. 5 Tablespoons (57.6g) of rose water (2 ounces)

Redaction:

Toast saffron threads on a dry griddle on low heat until it darkens (this will take just a few seconds) remove from heat and when it cools, grind in a mortar and set aside. Take a bowl and add your flour and break the butter into it with your fingers and add all the ingredients except the water, and mix. Add water in increments until mixture forms a ball, may take more or less than I used. Knead the dough a while and dust with a little flour when it starts to stick. You do not need to work the dough very much and you do not need to give it a rest because there is very little gluten in this flour. Divide dough in half and place a damp towel over the half you are not using. On a wooden surface, start rolling out the other half, try keeping it as much as possible in a circle, and dust it every now and then with a pinch of flour to keep it from sticking. Roll dough out thin, say between 1/8 to 3/8 inches thick. This will make a very large pie, say 12 or 14 inches in diameter, so I divided my dough into quarters and made two pies 8 ½ inches in diameter so I could taste one and bring one to freeze for a later time. When you have a circle of dough, fold in half and then fold again into a quarter and place half-way into your buttered pie pan and unfold, pressing carefully to the sides and bottom of the pan. If you have a gap, just take extra dough and press into the gap as this dough is very forgiving. Add around 3 and 1/2 cups of filling from the following pie recipes for the fruit and 4 cups for the meat pies. Roll out your top and seal it well to the bottom pastry. Place butter on top of pie, as the recipe will tell you, and cut three small slits in the center with a sharp knife to let out steam. Bake in 325 degree F oven for around an hour or until the pastry looks done (light brown) and a knife comes out clean when you test the middle of the pie. Rotate pie and change rack levels half way through the cooking time in case there are hot spots in the oven. Put sugar on top of pies when there is 5 or 10 minutes left in the cooking time. Take pies out and cool before slicing.

20D   TO MAKE A PIE IN THE GERMAN STYLE

They say nothing is more American than apple pie, but here we have a German apple pie in an Italian cookbook from 1549. Looks like apple pie has been around for a lot longer than we thought! One of the things I loved about this recipe was the shape of the apple slices, thick cut length wise. This will make a nice presentation when the pie is cut. This pie is about as decadent as you can make an apple pie, and is just wonderful to eat.

A FARE TORTE ALLA TEDESCHA.

PIGLIARAI Pome dolci fino a quindici, o vinti fecondo la grof fezza che ferano, e le mondarai, poi le tagliarai in fette honeftamente grandi, e le porrai in vn vafo con libra meza di zuccharo, e libra meza di Buttiero frefcho et acqua tanto che fiano quafi cotti, e ben dolci, poi li cauarai fuori con deftrez za fiche non fi rompino le fette, e le feruarai in vno Vafo, poi onta la Tiella con oncie due di Buttiero frefcho, li porrai fopra la tua fpoglia, con oncie quattro di zuccharo, et oncia meza di Canella fopra, e poi li diftenderai fopra le fette delle pome tanto, quanto tiene la fpoglia, e fopra dette fette li porrai oncie quattro di zuccharo grattato, et oncia meza di Canella, et oncie quattro di Buttiero fres fcho disfatto gettandolo in qua, e la a poco a poco, poi li porrai l'altra fpoglia fo pra con tre oncie di Buttiero frefcho disfatto, e la porrai a cuocere, a fuoco lento perche poco li bifogna a cuocere, e come fara cotta li porrai fopra oncie quattro di zuccharo.
    E in quefta Torta fi puote fare anche due o tre fuoli di Pome ponendoli trame zo Zuccharo e Canella.

You shall take fifteen or twenty good sweet apples, according to the size that they are, and you shall peel and core them, then you shall cut them lengthwise in grand slices, and you shall put them in a pot with a half-pound of sugar, and a half- pound of fresh butter, and water, so much that when it is nearly cooked it will be sweet.

Then you shall remove them outside with caution, so that you do not break the slices, and you shall serve up into a pot. Then grease a baking pan with two ounces of fresh butter, you shall put over your pastry sheet with four ounces of sugar over and a half-ounce of cinnamon. And then you shall spread over the apple slices so much that fill the pastry. And over named slices you shall put four ounces of grated sugar, and a half-ounce of cinnamon, and four ounces of melted butter, cast here and there little by little. Then you shall put over the other pastry sheet with three ounces of fresh melted butter.

And you shall put it to cook over a low fire, because little is needed to cook it, and when it is cooked, you shall put over it four ounces of sugar.

And in this pie you can also make two or three layers of apples, putting between them sugar and cinnamon.

Ingredients (pie filling)

1. Fifteen medium sized sweet apples (I used 'Pink Lady')
2. ¾ Cup (172.5g) of sugar (6 ounces)
3. 1 ½ Sticks (172.5g) of butter (6 ounces)
4. 1 Quart of water or enough to cover apple slices
5. 2 Ounces (57.6) of butter (one ounce for each baking pan)
6. 1 Ounce (28.8g) of ground true cinnamon (~7 tablespoons) divided into four equal parts
7. 1 Cup (172.5g) of sugar (8 ounces) divided into four equal parts
8. 1 Stick (115.2g) of melted butter (4 ounces) divided into two equal portions for the apple filling
9. 6 Tablespoons (86.4g) of melted butter (3 ounces) divided into two equal portions for top of pies
10. Four ounces (1/2 cup) (115.2g) of sugar divided into two equal portions for garnishing the pies

Redaction:

Peel and core fifteen medium sized apples (if they are small use twenty). Cut them crosswise into ½ inch or somewhat larger, as Christoforo says, to make them honestly into grand slices. When it is cut crosswise, you get a circular slice with a hole in the middle, very grand indeed! Place apple slices in a large pot and add ingredients 2 thru 4 and bring to the simmer and make sure apple slices are just covered with water, may take more than one quart. Bring the pot to the simmer for around 10 to 15 minutes until apple slices are cooked but can still hold their shape, and you must pay close attention to how much you cook them because they will disintegrate if they get too soft. When the apple slices are done, but still holding their shape, drain the slices in a colander carefully. The left over juice can be cooked down until it is thick and added later to the pie slices. This can be left out if you want to, as this is not in the recipe.

Make two batches of pastry from 19B. Roll out your pastry dough and divide into four pieces (the top pastry dough can be somewhat smaller than the bottom) as I made two pies of middle size, but Christoforo's recipe is for one large pie. I used two nine inch pie pans with a baking paper circle in the bottom with an ounce (two tablespoons) of melted butter in the bottom of each pan. Place a rolled out pastry sheet in the bottom of each pan and add ¼ cup of sugar to the bottom of each pan (ingredient 7) and spread it out evenly with a fourth part of ground cinnamon from ingredient 6. Place all the apple slices into the two pans carefully and add rest of sugar and cinnamon evenly over the top of the apple slices. If you are using it, add half of the boiled down juice from cooking the apples, and pour half of ingredient 8 butter on top of the apple slices, and place your pastry sheet top on each pie, and cut three slits into the pastry tops to allow steam to escape.   Place half (three tablespoons) of ingredient 9 butter over the top of each pie and place pies in a 350 degree F oven for around 40 to 50 minutes or until tops of the pastry are slightly brown. When pies are done, place a ¼ cup garnish sugar (ingredient 9) on top of each pie. You will note that these pies seem to take more cooking time than Christoforo says, but I think he was using a much larger, shallower baking pan that cooked much quicker.

22C   PIE OF MORELLO CHERRIES, OR RED CHERRIES, OR MULBERRIES, OR MELONS, OR FIGS

Next recipe is a fruit pie with many choices for the filling; I choose mulberries because you do not hear of this kind of pie very often. The most interesting ingredient is the use of a hard cheese with the fruit, I choose provolone, but a hard feta would be very good, as well. The trick here is to pick a not very dominating flavored hard cheese.

TORTA DI MARENE, O CERESE, O
More, o Melloni, o Fiche.

PIGLIA libre quattro di Marene, e falle cuocere nel vino bianco, e se sera dolce sera migliore, poi passale per la stamegna, e ponile in un vaso con libra una di Formaggio duro grattato, et oncie otto di zuccharo, & oncia una di cannella, & vn quarto di Peuere, e lib. 1. di Buttiero, & uoua sei, e incorpora bene ogni cosa insieme, poi empi le tue spoglie, e fa la Torta come è detto nell'altre, e ponli sopra oncie sei di Buttiero, poi la porrai a cuocere, e come sera quasi cotta, li darai oncie tre in quattro di zuccharo sopra, e poi la finirai di cuocere.
E al medesimo modo fara quelle delle Cerese, o More, le Fiche, esse non vanno cotte, ma soffritte in Buttiero, poi passale per la stamegna.

Take four pounds of Morello cherries, and make to cook in white wine, and if it shall be sweet, it shall be better. Then pass it through the cloth filter, and put it in a pan with a pound of hard cheese grated, and eight ounces of sugar, and an ounce of cinnamon, and a quarter (ounce) of pepper, and a pound of butter, and six eggs, and mix everything well together.

Then fill your pastry shells, and make a pie like it is named in the others, and put over six ounces of butter. Then you shall put it to cook, and when it shall be nearly cooked you shall give it three to four ounces of sugar on top, and then you shall finish with cooking it.

And in the same way you shall make those of the red cherries, or mulberries, the figs, they are not cooked, but fried in butter, then pass them through the cloth filter.

Ingredients
1. 11 Cups (1380g) of fresh mulberries (4 pounds)
2. 4 Cups of Moscato wine (I used Barefoot and Sutter Homes)
3. 3 and ½ Cups (345g) of shredded provolone cheese (1 pound)
4. 1 and 1/8 Cups (230g) of sugar (8 ounces)
5. 7 Tbs. (28.8g) of true cinnamon (1 ounce)
6. 1 Scant Tbs. (7.2g) of ground pepper (¼ ounce)
7. 3 Sticks (345g) of butter (1 pound)
8. 6 Eggs
9. 1 and ½ sticks (172.8g) of butter on top of pie before baking (6 ounces)
10. Scant ½ cup (86.4g) of sugar for top of pie when nearly done (3 ounces)

Redaction:
I had hoped to use fresh mulberries from my tree, but the birds ate them all, so I used dried mulberries soaked in water to cover overnight in a closed bowl in the fridge. Next day I measured out 11 cups of drained mulberries into a pot with four cups of sweet wine and simmered them for one hour uncovered. Drain mulberries when cool and boil down wine

residue until syrupy, watch that it does not scorch. Pound mulberries in a mortar or whiz in a food processor until crushed and pass thru a sieve; I used a ricer, which worked very well. Place mulberry pulp in a large bowl with wine residue, add ingredients 3 thru 8, and mix everything well together. Make your pie shells as it is stated in pastry recipe 19B, which gives you enough dough to make a 12-14 inch pie, but I choose to make two 8 ½ inch pies. Fill your pie or pies, cover with the top shell and place ingredient 9 butter on top, and cut three slits to let out steam. Bake in a 325 degree F oven for around an hour, or until crusts turn golden brown. It is a good idea to rotate pies and change levels half way thru the cooking time in case there are hot spots in the oven. Place ingredient 10 sugar on top of pies when there are 5 or 10 minutes left in the baking time, and finish baking them.

22D   PIE OF MEDLARS, OR PEACHES, OR PEARS, OR APPLES, OR CHESTNUTS, OR ACORNS, OR WATER CHESTNUTS, OR QUINCES, OR OF OTHERS

This next recipe has a lot of choices for the filling, and one of the most interesting is the Italian word tregoli, which is misspelled in the title and should be trigoli. Emilio Faccioil in the *Arte Della Cucina* says it is water chestnuts, but John Florio says it is a type of cardoon or thistle or artichoke in his Italian dictionary *Queen Anna's New World* of *Words*. My inclination is to go with water chestnuts as it fits better with the other ingredients, but this may not be right.

TORTA DI NESPILE, O PERSICHE,
O PERF, O POME, O CASTA,
gnᵉ, o Giande, o Tregoli, o Co‑
dogne, od'altro.

PIGLIA Le Nespile matture, e falle cuocere in brodo grasso, poi pas‑
sale per la stamegna, e ponile in vn Vaso con libra vna di Formaggio duro grat
tato, & oncie noue di zuccharo, & oncia vna di Canella pista, & un quarto di
Peuere, e meza libra di Buttiero, e Voua tre, e incorpora bene ogni cosa insie‑
me, & empi le tue spoglie, e fa la Torta, e poi poneli sopra oncie quattro di But‑
tiero fresco, e ponla a cuocere, e come sera cotta li porrai sopra oncie tre in quat‑
tro di zuccharo fino. E'l medemo ordine seruarai in quelle di Persiche, o Pere, o
Pome. Ma in quelle di Castagne, o Giande, o Tregoli, dopoi che queste cose se
rano cotte, le pistarai nel Mortaio, e distemperate con brodo, le passarai per la sta
megna giongēdoli le robbe che hai fatto nelle altre, eccetto che del Buttiero, che
hai posto nelle altre di libra meza, in queste ne porrai libra vna, e dopoi sopra, ne
porrai libra meza, & auuertissi che le Giande vogliono essere fresche, e non sec‑
che, & ne i giorni che non serano da carne, le potrai cuocere nell'acqua con But‑
tiero in cambio del brodo.
Ma le Nespile, Pere, Pome, Persiche, e Codogne, stariano meglio cotte in Vi
no dolce, o Sabba, e posso anche cuocersi sotto le bragie, io ti propongo molti
partiti accio che pigli quello che ti piace.

Take the mature medlars, and make to cook in rich broth, then pass them through the cloth filter, and put them in a pot with a pound of grated hard cheese, and nine ounces of sugar, an ounce of pounded cinnamon, and a quarter (ounce) of pepper, and a half-pound of butter, and three eggs, and mix everything well together. And fill your pastry shells and make the pie and then put over it four ounces of fresh butter, and put it to cook.

When it shall be cooked you shall put over it three to four ounces of fine (ground) sugar. And the same method you shall keep in those of peaches, or pears, or apples, but in those of chestnuts, or acorns, or water chestnuts, then when these things are cooked, you shall pound them in the mortar, and dilute with broth, you shall pass them through the cloth filter, add the things that you have done in the others, except that of the butter, since you have placed a half-pound in the others, in these with it you shall put a pound, and then over it you shall put a half-pound. And notice that that the acorns need to be fresh and not dry, and with it in the days that shall not be of meat, you can cook it in water with butter in exchange of the broth.

But the medlars, pears, apples, peaches, and quinces are better cooked in sweet wine, or cooked wine must, and can also be cooked under the coals.

I proposed many solutions so that you take those that you want.

Ingredients

1. 15 Ripe peaches
2. Two cups of sweet wine (I used Elysium or a red sweet wine)
3. 6 ¾ Cups (345g) of grated hard cheese (I used Greek mizithra)
4. 1 and 1/8 Cups (259.2g) of sugar (nine ounces)
5. 7 Tablespoons (28.8g) of ground true cinnamon (one ounce)
6. One tablespoon and ¼ teaspoon (7.2g) of fresh ground black pepper (1/4 ounce)
7. One and a half sticks (172.5g) of melted butter (six ounces)
8. 3 Eggs
9. One stick (175.2g) of melted butter divided in half for top of each pie before baking (four ounces)
10. Six tablespoon (86.4g) of sugar divided in half for to garnish top of pies after baking (three ounces)

Redaction:

Take the ripe peaches and cut into chunks, removing the pit. Place in a large pan with a heavy bottom and add wine. Bring to the simmer, cover with a lid, and simmer slowly for ten minutes or so until they are very soft, and when the peaches are very soft and very thick, sieve them through loose cheese cloth to remove the skins or use a metal fruit sieve, as I used. You will have to use a small amount at a time and clean the sieve periodically from the skins to keep from clogging the sieve. Pace sieved mixture into a large bowl and stir ingredients 3 thru 8 into it and mix very well. Roll out your pastry dough from recipe 19B and note that I am making two nine inch pies instead of one large pie as Christoforo says in the recipe. You can use a little more of the pastry dough for the bottom of the pies than the tops. It is a good idea to put a baking paper circle in the bottom of the pans and grease the paper and pan with butter. When you put the tops on, take your fingers and run them around the edges to seal the pie and make it look more attractive. Cut three slits in the top and pour over ingredient 9 butter and place in a 350 degree F oven for around one hour and twenty or thirty minutes or until the pie tops are slightly brown. As in the apple pie, I think Christoforo is using a much larger shallower pie pan to fix his pie, which would cook faster. When pie is ready, place ingredient 10 sugar over each pie and they are ready to serve when they cool.

23B RESTORED PIE OF FLESH OF CAPON OR OF MEAT OF VEAL

Here we have a capon or veal pie with lots of spices, cheese, nuts, fruit and lots of butter and fat. This is very rich and filling, and who does not like a hot meat pie? The meat I chose was veal, which is expensive as well as capon, but chicken will work especially for a large feast.

TORTA DI POLPE DE CAPPONI, O DI Carne di Vitello, restaurativa.

PRIMA Pigliarai le polpe de Capponi, et anche le coscie et altra parte che sia buona da pistar' ouero, Carne di cossetto di Vitello, o l'uno e l'altro c. lcato, e lo pistara molto bene nel Mortaio con tre, o quattro fette di pan mogliato in brodo, con libra una di Pignuoli mondi, e libra una di Morolla di bue, ouero, libra una di grasso, non potendo hauer' morolla, lequali cose tutte ben piste insieme distemperarai con poco brodo e passarai per la stamegna, e le ponerai in un vaso, poi li aggiungerai libra meza di Formaggio grasso grattato, e libra meza di buon Formaggio di parmezana od'altra sorte simile grattato, et uoua dodici et oncia una di Canella fina, et un sesto di Peuere et un picicotto di gengeuro, et un poco di zaffrano, et oncie tre d'uua passa ben lauata e monda, e ogni cosa incorporarai ben insieme, con libra meza di zuccharo, et oncie tre d'Acqua rosa, e farai la tua Torta seruando l'ordine che hai seruato nelle altre, ponendoli il zuccharo sopra a tempo, e il Buttiero.

First you shall take flesh of capons and also the legs, and other parts that are good to grind, or veal leg meat, or one or the other, boiled.

And you shall pound it very well in the mortar with three or four slices of bread soaked in broth, with a pound of shelled pine nuts, and a pound of beef marrow, or a pound of fat when you are not able to have marrow. As all things are well pounded together you shall dilute with a small amount of broth and you shall pass it through the cloth filter, and you shall put it in a pan.

Then you shall add a half-pound of fatty grated cheese, and a half-pound of good Parmesan cheese grated or other similar kinds, and twelve eggs, and a ounce of fine (pounded) cinnamon, and a sixth (ounce) of pepper, and a pinch of ginger, and a small amount of saffron, and three ounces of well washed and seeded raisins. And you shall mix everything well together, with a half-pound of sugar, and three ounces of rose water.

And you shall make your pie attending to the method that you have served in the others; putting the sugar over in time, and the butter.

Ingredients

1. 2 and 2/3 pounds (747.6g) or two avoirdupois pounds of lean veal, cubed. I used veal shoulder meat
2. Four slices of good white bread
3. Veal broth
4. 2 ¾ Cups (345g) of pine nuts (1 pound)
5. 1 ½ Cups (345g) of pounded beef fat or beef marrow (1 pound)
6. 1 ½ Cups (172.5g) of freshly grated Provolone cheese (½ pound)
7. ~Six cups (172.5g) of freshly grated Parmesan cheese (½ pound)
8. 12 Eggs, well beaten
9. ~Four tablespoons (28.8g) of true cinnamon (If you grind it in a coffee grinder, it is much fluffier and will take ~7 tablespoons) (1 ounce)
10. Two somewhat generous teaspoons (4.8g) of freshly ground black pepper (1/6 ounce)
11. Pinch of ginger
12. Pinch of saffron
13. Generous ½ cup (86.4g) of raisins (3 ounces)
14. ¾ Cup (172.5g) of sugar (½ pound)
15. Six Tablespoons (86.4g) of rose water (3 ounces)
16. One stick (115.2g) of melted butter (4 ounces) (half stick for the top of each pie before baking)
17. Three ounces (86.4g) of sugar (1/3 cup) (~three tablespoons for to garnish top of each pie after baking.)

Redaction:

Place the veal in a pot and just cover with water and bring to the simmer on the stove and cover with a lid. Simmer slowly for forty minutes, and cool. Remove the veal cubes with a slotted spoon, and soak the slices of bread in the leftover veal broth for ten minutes or so, and pound the veal cubes in a mortar with a pestle (a whole lot of work!) or whiz in the food processor for a few seconds with the drained bread slices, pine nuts, and beef fat. Do not over blend or you will turn it into baby food! Place the blended mixture into a large bowl and add cheeses, eggs, cinnamon, pepper, spices, raisins, sugar and rose water, and mix very well.

Make your pastry dough (recipe 19 B) and prepare your pie pans just like the apple and peach pies and bake in a 350 degree F oven for one hour and twenty minutes or until the top pastry crust is somewhat brown. As in the others, I am baking two pies with the recipe while Christoforo is baking one. Don't forget to place the butter on top of each pie before baking and add garnish sugar after baking.

23D TO MAKE A PIE OF FRESH GOURDS OR MULBERRIES, OR SOUR CHERRIES

This next pie I choose cherries as the ingredient instead of gourds or mulberries. In my translation, I have found six different types of cherries grown in Ferrara in the 16th century, but I cannot tell the variety of the cherry except wild cherries. The way these fruit are used indicates that most varieties were sour rather than sweet. This is, as you can tell, a very rich pie with all that butter!

A FARE TORTA DI ZVCCHE, fresche, o More, o Marine.

PIGLIARAI le zucche, auuertendo che nõ siano amare e le mondarai e grattarei come faresti il formaggio, e poi le porrai a bogliere in buono brodo grasso, con libra una di Morolla di bue, o di grasso di Manzo, ma non uuole troppo bogliere, e le passarai per la stamegna, e porrai in un vaso, cõ libra vna di Formaggio duro grattato, e due Pouine, & uoua sei, & un Bicchiero di latte, e libra meza di Zuccharo, & oncia meza di Canella, & un quarto di Peuere, e di gengeuro mezo quarto, & un poco di Zaffrano, e mescolarai bene ogni cosa insieme poi farai la tua Torta, e come sara fatta li porrai sopra oncie quattro di Buttiero, e la porrai a cuocere, e come sera quasi cotta, li porrai sopra oncie tre in quattro di Zuccharo, e poi la finirai di cuocere, & i giorni che non sono da carne farai cuocere le Zucche nell'acqua con Buttiero, ouero nel latte, e in vece della Morolla, o grasso, li porrai Buttiero.

Auuertendo che tutte le sopradette Torte sono conueniente honestamente per ogni gran Prencipe, & a conuiti, e ad'altro, ma per l'ordinario con poco piu della meta della Spitiaria si farebbono, e seriano giudicate buone.

You shall take gourds, note that they are not bitter, and you shall peel and you shall grate them like you would do the cheese. And then you shall put them to boil in good rich broth, with a pound of beef marrow, or with fat of a young steer, but it does not need too much boiling. And you shall pass through the cloth filter and you shall put in a pot with a pound of hard grated cheese, and two ricottas (cheeses), and six eggs, and a glass (~4 ounces) of milk, and a half-pound of sugar, and a half-ounce of cinnamon, and a quarter (ounce) of pepper, and a half-quarter (ounce) of ginger (i.e. 1/8 ounce), and a small amount of saffron. And you shall mix everything well together. Then you shall make your pie, and when it is made you shall put over it four ounces of butter, and you shall put it to cook, and when it is nearly cooked, you shall put over it three to four ounces of sugar, and then you shall finish cooking it.

And on days that are not of meat you shall make to cook the gourds in the water with butter, or in milk, and instead of marrow or fat, you shall put butter.

Notice that all the above-mentioned pies are honestly suitable for every great prince, and for feasts, and for others, in fact for the ordinary, withal a little more than half of the special ones would be made, and they shall be judged good. *

* Messisbugo is referring to the first recipe, 19B, which gives two ways of making piecrusts, the ordinary and the refined.

Ingredients

1. Four cans (around 1380g of drained cherries) of tart cherries in water
2. 3 Sticks of butter (345g) (1 pound)
3. 3 ½ Cups (345g) of shredded provolone cheese (1 pound)
4. 1 Cup (230.4g) of ricotta cheese (my best guess)
5. Six eggs
6. ½ Cup of milk (my best guess)
7. ¾ Cup (172.5g) of sugar (½ pound)
8. 3 ½ Tbs. (14.4g) of ground true cinnamon (½ ounce)
9. Scant Tbs. (7.2g) of ground pepper (¼ ounce)
10. Scant tsp. (3.6g) of ginger paste (1/8 ounce)
11. Pinch of saffron
12. 1 Stick (115.2g) of butter on top of pie before baking (4 ounces)
13. Scant ½ cup (86.4g) of sugar for top of pie when nearly done (3 ounces)

Redaction:

Place four cans of cherries with their juice in a pan and add the 3 sticks of butter and simmer for 20 minutes. Remove the cherries with a slotted spoon and boil down cherry juice and butter until it becomes much reduced in volume. Pound cherries in a mortar or whiz in a food processor until pulped. When reduced cheery juice and butter is cooled, sieve the cherry pulp and juice thru a metal or cheese cloth sieve and place in a large pan with ingredients 3 thru 11 and mix very well. Make your pies or pie just like the mulberry pie, but note that Christoforo only wants 1 stick of butter on top before baking instead of 1 ½ sticks for the mulberry pie. I did two pies instead of one, as in the mulberry pie, so use half of ingredient 12 butter on each pie and half of the sugar garnish (ingredient 13) on each pie for the last 5-10 minutes of cooking.

Chapter 3

Paste Per Di Di Quaresima, Gran Vigilie, Delle Qualianche Se Ne Puote Servire Per Tramezi Ne Gli Altri Giorni
(Pastry for the Day of Lent and Grand Vigil, of These You can Serve for the Middle (of Feast) and for Other Days)

25D TO MAKE TEN PLATTERS OF SMALL FRITTERS, OF MARZIPAN, OR TEN SMALL PIES

When I was translating this next recipe, I was stunned to see the ratio of three pounds almonds to one pound of sugar, for most cookbooks in period use a one pound of almonds to one pound of sugar. A 1to1 ratio will give you a good molding type of marzipan, but this one is for taste, and what a taste it is! It is hard to decide which one is better, the small pies or the fritters, try them both and see what you think.

A FARE DIECI PIATI DI PASTATELLE, DI MARZAPANE,
ouero dieci Tortelle.

PIGLIA Libre tre di Mandole ambrosine, e pellale, poi pistale nel Mortaio con libra vna di zuccharo, e oncie tre d'acqua rosata, e oncie vna di Canella, e vn quarto di Peuere, e pista bene ogni cosa insieme; Poi piglia lib. tre di Farina biancha, e otto Torli d'Voua, et di zuccharo oncie quattro, et di Buttiero, ouero dileguito oncie quattro, et d'acqua rosata oncie tre, e vn poco de Zaffrano, e fanne vna pasta, poi fa la tua spoglia sottile quanto sia possibile; Poi piglia del detto battuto tanto quanto sia vna noce, e vallo distendendo sopra detta spoglia; Poi voltarai la spoglia ch'e disotto disopra, e la premerai con le mani, e la tagliarai poi colla speronella, ouero il bussolo, si che siano tōde e li farai vno rotellino d'intorno come si farebbe a vna Tortella; Poi habbi libre quattro di Dileguito, ouero buon Buttiero, e frigele, e poi le imbandirai dieci per piatello, e li porrai sopra fra tutte oncie sei di zuccharo.

Take three pounds of peeled sweet almonds, then grind in the mortar with a pound of sugar, and three ounces of rose water, and a ounce of cinnamon, and a quarter (ounce) of pepper, and grind everything well together.

Then take three pounds of white flour, and eight egg yolks, and four ounces of sugar, and four ounces of butter or lard, and three ounces of rose water, and a small amount of saffron, and make pastry dough.

Then make your pastry sheets as thin as possible. Then take of the named mixture so much as to be one walnut, and vigorously spread over the pastry sheet.

Then you shall fold the pastry sheet so that the bottom is on top, and you will press them with the hands, and you shall cut it with the pastry cutter, or round pastry can cutter, so that it is round, and you shall make a small wheel around like it would be made in a pie.

Then take four pounds of lard, or good butter, and fry, and then you shall ready them for the banquet ten per small plate, and you shall put over between all of them six ounces of sugar.

Ingredients
Pastry
1. 6 ¾ Cups (1035g) of soft wheat flour (3 pounds)
2. 8 Egg yolks
3. ½ Cup (115.2g) of sugar (4 ounces)
4. 1 Stick (4 ounces, 115.2g) of butter (4 ounces)
5. 6½ Tbs. (86.4g) of rose water (3 ounces)
6. Pinch of ground saffron
7. 13 Tbs. of water (this will vary)

Filling
1. ~7 Cups (1035g) of peeled almonds (3 pounds)
2. 1½ Cups (345g) of sugar (1 pound)
3. 6½ Tbs. (86.4g) of rose water (3 ounces)
4. 7 Tbs. (28.8g) of ground true cinnamon (1 ounce)
5. 1 Tbs. (¼ ounce, 7.2g) of ground black pepper (¼ ounce)
6. A few drops of water to stop the oiling effect

Garnish
1. ¾ Cup (172.5g) of sugar (6 ounces)

Redaction:

For the pastry, take a large bowl and add all of the egg yolks and beat until they are thick, and then slowly add sugar until the mixture forms the ribbon and is a pale yellow color. Then beat in rose water and saffron and start adding water until dough forms a ball. Take the dough and knead a bit so that it is well mixed. Do not worry about letting the dough rest as it has such low gluten content it does not need it. If you have a large mixer like a K5A or 6 quart Kitchen Aid you can use the baffle attachment to mix the ingredients and when it gets too stiff switch to the dough hook attachment and finish mixing it. This is a large recipe, so the machine sure does help out.

For the filling, take large pan half way filled with water and bring to the boil and add the almonds, bring back to the boil, and boil for one minute. Remove from heat and add cold water, and you should be able to slip the skins off the almonds with your fingers. I then filled my food processor (14 cup) about 1/3 full and pulsed them carefully for a few seconds, adding drops of rose water every now and then to stop the oiling effect. You must pay close attention to this problem. When the almonds are minced fairly well, add them to a large bowl and fill the food processor up again to the 1/3 level, and repeat this procedure until all the almonds are minced. Add the sugar and spices to the almonds and mix very well and again fill the food processor 1/3 full with this mixture, and pulse it adding rose water (note: if you run out, use water) every now and then. You will have to stop every now and then to move the mixture inside the bowl so that the blades can engage it. After a while the mixture will collect into a ball (hold the machine down), run the machine for a few more seconds and you have marzipan! Repeat this procedure until all the mixture is made into marzipan. The key here is to not overload the food processor and to watch the oiling effect. In period, they would have used a large mortar and pestle and a lot of back breaking work to make this much marzipan!

The title of the recipe says you can make ten platters of marzipan fritters with ten fritters per platter or ten small pies. So I decided to make some pies first. Take a three or four inch piece (more or less) of pastry dough and roll it out with a rolling pin on a floured pastry board as thin as you can get it. Fold into quarters and place into an eight inch pie pan that has a buttered paper disk in the bottom, and unfold the pastry sheet. Press it all around with your hands to make the bottom shell, and fill with marzipan to around an inch thick, or more if you want, and take another small ball of dough and make a top for the pie. There is enough dough to make several pies, and if you want ten pies I think you will have to use a six inch pie pan or smaller. Place this dough on top of the pie and pinch the top dough onto the bottom dough so that the pie is well enclosed with dough. Cut three slits on top with a sharp knife to let out steam, place in a preheated 350F degree oven and bake for 30 minutes or until lightly brown. Remove from oven, place a tablespoon of garnish sugar all over the pie, and place back in oven for 5 minutes. Remove from oven and let cool for an hour before cutting it.

To make the fritters, I took a six or seven inch ball of dough and rolled it out into a thin rectangle (or as close as you can). The hard part seems to be in getting it thin. Next I rolled small walnut seized balls of marzipan and placed them two or three inches apart over half of the dough sheet and then pushed down over each marzipan ball too flatten it a little. Place the empty part of the sheet over the other part and press very well with your hands all around the flatten marzipan balls and cut a circle around the filling with a pastry wheel. Make sure they are closed up tight so they do not burst in the hot lard, press down hard with the pastry wheel. I used an electric deep fat fryer set on 375F degrees with seven cups of rendered pork lard, and added four fritters to the lard with a basket, and cooked them for two minutes. As you can see, they cook very quickly, so when they turn a light brown and start to float they are done. Place them on a paper towel.

When you have ten fritters done and drained and still warm, sprinkle a generous tablespoon of garnish sugar over them.

27B   TO MAKE TEN PLATTERS OF LENTEN DAINTY CHEWETS

This recipe is for people with a sweet tooth. It has got it all, with sugar, spices, honey, and sweet wine with browned almond slivers. This finished dish would make a spectacular presentation when served at a banquet, and is a great representative renaissance dish. The tough part is getting the dough through the back side of a grater. Ff you have trouble, try using the sharp side with caution. The other thing that may help is grating the dough directly into the hot oil.

A FARE DIECI PIATI DI Frilengotti Magri

PIGLIA Di Farina biancha libre due e meza, e oncia meza di Gengeuro, e oncia vna di Canella, e vn quarto di Peuere, e vn ottauo de Garofali, e meza libra di Zuccharo, e d'Acqua rosa oncie due, e vn poco di zaffrano, e oncie tre d'Olio, e vn Bicchiero di Vin biancho, e se e dolce e meglio, e cosi impasta dette cose insieme, e fanne vna pasta che sia piu duretta, che non e quella de i Maccheroni; Poi fa i frilengotti, togliendo tanta pasta quanto e vna grossa castagna, menandoli sopra il rouerscio della grattugia; Poi frigele in Olio, poi piglia vna libra di Mandole colla gussa, e falle brustellare in vna patella sopra la cenere calda, e poi lasciale rafredare; Poi metti i Frilengotti in vn Vaso, come sono cotti, con libre due di Mele; Poi taglia le dette Mandole alla longa minute, e mettile in detto Vaso, e mescola molto bene sotto sopra, accio che le Mandole vadino in ogni parti; Poi l'imbandirai ne i piati, ponendoli sopra oncie sei di zuccharo, e oncia meza di Canella.

Take two and a half-pounds of white flour, and a half-ounce of ginger, and a ounce of cinnamon, and a quarter-(ounce) of pepper, and one eighth-(ounce) of cloves, and a half- pound of sugar, and two ounces of rose water, and a small amount of saffron, and three ounces of oil, and one wine-glassful (~ 4 ounces) of white wine and if it is sweet it is better, and knead these named things together, and make a pastry dough which is quite hard, but not as is that of the macaroni (recipe 11D).

Then make the chewets, remove so much pastry dough as to be as much as a large chestnut spreading it over the backside of the grater. Then fry them in oil. Then take a pound of almonds with the skin and put to brown in a pan over the hot ashes, and then let them cool.

Then put the chewets in a pan, when they are cooked, with two pounds of honey, then cut the named almonds in thin lengthwise slices, and put in named bowl, and mix very well underneath and above, so that the almonds go to all the parts.

Then you shall ready it for the banquet in the platters, putting over six ounces of sugar, and a half-ounce of cinnamon.

Ingredients
1. 6 ¼ Cups (862.5g) of soft wheat flour (2 ½ pounds)
2. Scant tablespoon (14.4g) of ginger paste (½ ounce)
3. 6 Tablespoons (28.8g) of ground true cinnamon (1 ounce)
4. 1 ½ Tablespoons (7.2g) of ground black pepper (¼ ounce)
5. 1 ½ Teaspoons (3.6g) of ground cloves (1/8 ounce)
6. ¾ Cup (172.5g) of sugar (½ pound)
7. 4 Tablespoons plus one teaspoon (57.6g) of rose water (2 ounces)
8. Pinch of ground saffron
9. 8 ½ Tablespoons (86.4g) of olive oil (3 ounces)
10. ½ Cup (100.8g) of sweet white wine (I used a Sutters Home Moscato) (4 ounces)
11. ~14 Tablespoons of water (this may vary)
12. 1.7 Liters of olive oil for frying

Garnish

1. 2 Cups (690g) of honey (2 pounds)
2. 2 ¼ Cups (345g) of browed skinned almonds sliced lengthwise (1 pound)
3. ¾ Cup (172.5g) of sugar (½ pound)
4. 3 ½ Tablespoons (14.4g) of ground true cinnamon (½ ounce)

Redaction:

    Mix dry ingredients in a large bowl, then add ginger paste (better to use ginger powder, but this what I had on hand), oil, wine and rose water. Add water a few tablespoons at a time until you get fairly thick dough. You may need more or less water than I used. When dough is well mixed, take a piece as large as a large chestnut, as Christoforo says, and rub it on the backside of a cheese grater in the basket that is used in the deep fat fryer, and cook in 375 degree F olive oil for 1-2 minutes or until they brown a bit, and drain well on a paper towel. I used a deep fat fryer that holds 1.7 Liters of olive oil, and it worked great. While pastry is cooling, place almonds in enough boiling water to cover and boil one minute and then drain them. When cool, slip off skins with your fingers, place almonds on a large cookie sheet and brown them in a 350 degree F oven for 10 minutes or so, watch that they do not burn or get too brown and, when cool, slice almonds lengthwise or just give them a rough chop. Place cooled pastry in a large bowl, add honey and mix very well. Add almond slivers and mix them in, as well. Place mixture on a nice platter and cast garnish sugar on top and then the garnish cinnamon on top of that. This is now ready for the banquet.

Chapter 4

Minestre, Da Grasso, E Magro
(Pottages for a Day of Meat and for Lent)

37C FRENCH CUSTARD SAUCE FOR FILLING FLEUR-DE-LIS, SACRED COWLS OF ST. JACOB'S FRITTERS AND CASES FOR PIES, FOR SOUP AND OTHERS

This one and the bread recipe are my favorite ones in the cookbook. I was blown away when I translated this, for it is a heavy custard sauce and it says in the French style. I don't know if that is true or not, but I have reason to think that 16th century Italian cooking influenced French cooking greatly. There are 15 recipes in the *Banchetti* that are stated in the French style, the most of any nation. I wish Christoforo had given precise measurements, but I think my redaction is fairly close. This has many ways of using the custard.

CREMA ALLA FRANCESE, PER EMPIRE FIORDELIGI, CAPPE SANTE DI SAN GIACOMO, TORtelle, e Casse da Pastelli, e per Minestra & altro.

PRIMA pigliarai del latte secondo la quantita di che le vorai fare, et voua ben battute, e zucc. Poi piglierà farina bianca con la metà del detto Latte e distemperarai bene ogni cosa con la detta Compositione, Poi pigliarai l'altra meta del Latte, e la ponerai in vn Vaso netto sopra la fiama del Fuoco ben chiara che non pigli fumo con buon Buttiero fresco, e come bogliera, li gettarai dentro la detta Compositione, menandola molto bene con un bastone larghetto dal capo disotto, e li gettarai dentro vn poco d'acqua rosata secódo la quantita che farai, e come vederai che sia stretta, la leuarai dal Fuoco, e la gettarai in vno altro Vaso, Poi potrai empire le paste sopra dette, e darle per Minestra con zuccharo Canella sopra.

First you will take milk according to the quantity of it you want to make, eggs well beaten and sugar. Then you will take white flour with half of the above milk and you will dissolve everything well together with the above composition. Then you will take the other half of the milk and you will put it in one clean pot over the flame of the fire well clear so that it does not take smoke with good fresh butter, and when boiling, you will put inside the above mixture, stirring very well with a wide stick from top to underneath, and you will place inside a small amount of rosewater according to the quantity that you will make, and when you see that it is thick you will remove it from the fire, and you will place it in another pot. Then you will put it to fill the pastries mentioned above, and to put in soup with sugar and cinnamon over.

Ingredients

1. 4 Cups of milk (divided)
2. 8 Large eggs
3. 1 ½ Cups of sugar
4. 1 Cup of soft wheat flour (~120g)
5. ¾ Quarter stick of butter
6. 3 Tablespoons of rose water

Redaction:

Place eggs in a mixing bowl or the bowl of a large mixer (I used a 6 quart Kitchen Aid) and mix them very well with a whip or a whip attachment. Then slowly add sugar until the egg and sugar mixture forms the ribbon. Next, slowly add half of the milk and mix very well and then carefully add the flour in small batches until the whole mixture is well mixed. You may want to switch to the baffle attachment when you add the flour. Take the other half of the milk with the butter and rose water, place in a medium heavy bottomed pan, and heat on medium high heat while stirring with a wooden spoon or a wooded spatula, as Christoforo says. Carefully bring mixture to the simmer and then add other milk, egg and flour mixture to the pan. Heat while stirring very well until mixture thickens, which will take a while and will form lumps, but as you keep stirring they will go away. When mixture is boiling and very thick, reduce heat and cook for two or three minutes while stirring to cook the flour, remove from heat, and it is ready. If it looks like it has scorched a little, transfer to another pot and let cool.

This recipe is very close to the crème patissiere in Julia Child's volume one cookbook, *Mastering The Art of French Cooking*. The only difference is Julia uses egg yolks and vanilla and Christoforo uses whole eggs and rose water. Another link to early modern cooking!

39E TO MAKE CRUSHED CHICKPEAS WITH PORK RIND

This next recipe has a very modern feel to it, and would be inexpensive to make for a large feast. This is very rich and very filling, as well. It has lots of pork fat and rind with herbs and spices, a nice dish on a cold day.

A FARE CESI ENFRANTI, CON CODEGHE.

PIGLIA i tuoi Cesi mondi e netti, e lauali con acqua di po, ouero di fiume, e poneli a cuocere in detta acqua, e cosi come si vano cuocendo, aggiun geli buon o brodo grasso, e poi piglia vna buona pestata di Lardo, e gettagliela dentro a cuocere, e fa che sia ben pesta, e poi piglia le tue codeghe cotte allesso da sua posta, e tagliale in quadretti, e gettagliele dentro con herbe oliose ehe sian ben peste con i coltelli, e fa che li sia sopra il tutto della menta, o verde, o secca in pol uere, e Peuere, e Gengeuro, e poi l'imbandirai.

Take your shelled chickpeas and clean, and wash with water of the Po, or river, and put them to cook in named water. And these when they are to be cooked, add good rich broth, and then take a good pounded (lump) of lard and cast it inside to cook, and make that they are well ground.

And then take your pork rind boiled cooked in its place, and cut it into four squares, and cast it inside with herbs in oil that are well pounded with the knives. And make that mint is over all of it, either green or dried, in powder, and pepper, and ginger, and then you shall ready it for the banquet.

Ingredients:
1. 1 Avoirdupois pound (454g) of dried chickpeas
2. 1 Quart of free range chicken broth (I used Pacific brand)
3. 1 Teaspoon of beef base (I used Minors brand)
4. 1 Teaspoon of vegetable base (I used Minors brand)
5. ¼ Cup of pork lard
6. 1.6 Avoirdupois pounds (726g) of jowl bacon
7. 1 Tablespoon of minced mint
8. ½ Tablespoon of minced oregano
9. ½ Tablespoon of minced bush basil
10. 2 Tablespoons of virgin olive oil
11. ½ Teaspoon of freshly ground black pepper
12. 1 Teaspoon of crushed ginger

Redaction:

Rinse chickpeas with cold water several times and put them to soak in eight cups of water overnight. Place jowl bacon (you can use a much smaller piece, but this was all I could find with rind on it) in a medium pot, cover with water, and boil cook for four hours or until very tender. Make sure it stays covered with simmering water at all times and when done, cool and store bacon and water in fridge overnight.

The next day, you can skim fat off the bacon broth with a spoon. Cut jowl bacon into four equal pieces and reserve. Drain off soaking water from the chickpeas and rinse several times with cool water. Place chickpeas in a large pot and add chicken broth, beef and vegetable base, and pork fat. Bring to the simmer for two hours, always adding extra hot water to keep them well covered. When nearly done, heat up jowl bacon and broth. When chickpeas are done, crush them in a mortar and pestle or whiz them in a food processor using the broth to release the blades when needed. Add crushed chickpeas with their broth back to the pan and add hot bacon broth with the four pieces of bacon to the pan and heat everything up until it simmers. I aimed for a thick soup-like consistency. If it is too thick add more hot water, and too thin simmer until it thickens. Shut off heat and add ingredients 7 through 12 to the pot, give a quick stir and it is ready to serve.

Chapter 5

Minestre Pre Di Di Quarsima O Gran Vigilie, Magre In Tutto
(Pottages for the Day of Lent or Grand Vigil, All Lenten)

42A TO MAKE LENTILS IN SAUCE

I now give you a lentil dish that is very good and healthy. Notice in the dish how he talks about the sweet and the sour, which is one of the things in the renaissance that you will see time and time again. The idea is to have a balance between the two, neither too sweet nor too sour, and an easy dish to fix for a banquet.

A FARE LENTE IN SAPORE

PIGLIA Vua passa, e nettala molto bene, e ponila in vn Mortaio, e pestala molto bene con pane ben brustellato che sia stato ammoglio nel Vino nero e vn poco d'Aceto insieme, e pesta bene el detto pane, e l'Vua passa, Poi distempera ogni cosa con detto Vino, e Aceto, e passa per lo setazzo, e come hai passate queste cose, ponile in vn vaso con Mele, tanto ch'habbi del dolce, e acetoso, Poi Canella, e Peuere, e ponile sopra il fuoco, che boglia adagio, mescolando questa compositione con vna Cazzolla fino atanto che veda che sia honestamente spessa. Dopoi piglia la tua Lente scolata che sia cotta nell'acqua, e mettila a bogliere in detto sapore vn pochetto, e sera fatto.

Take raisins and seed them very well, and put them in a mortar and grind them very well with well-toasted bread, which have been soaking in red wine and a small amount of vinegar together. And grind well the named bread and raisins, and then dissolve everything with named wine and vinegar and pass through the sieve.

And when you have pureed these things, you shall put it in a pot with honey, enough that you have some sweet and sour, then cinnamon and pepper, and put it over the fire, and boil slowly mixing this composition with a spatula, until to such a point that you would see that it is modestly thick. Afterwards take your sieved lentils that have been cooked in water, and put to boil in named sauce a little while, and it is done.

Ingredients

1. ½ Cup of golden raisins (other kinds are fine, too)
2. 1 Slice of well toasted white bread
3. 2 Cups of red wine (I used Apothic Red)
4. ½ Cup of good red wine vinegar
5. ¼ Cup of honey
6. 1 Tablespoon of ground true cinnamon
7. ¾ Teaspoon of ground black pepper
8. 1 Avoirdupois pound of brown lentils
9. 1 Teaspoon of salt (I added this as I am sure they put some salt in the dish)

Redaction:

Grind raisins in a mortar and pestle or whiz in food processor. Soak slice of bread in wine and vinegar for 20 minutes. Grind the bread mixture with the raisins and sieve through a metal colander. I added a cup of water to get the mixture through the sieve; you can use a little more if you need to, as the sauce will be concentrated by boiling on the stove. When everything is well sieved, add the mixture to a good non-corrosive pot and add honey and the spices and salt. Boil slowly while stirring with a spatula until it is modestly thick, and then remove from the fire and set aside.

In another pot, bring your washed lentils together with 6 cups of water to the slow simmer, and simmer them for 25 minutes. Drain the lentils in a colander and add them to the other pot with the sauce and simmer them together for 5 minutes, taste for salt and they are done.

42D   TO MAKE A POTTAGE OF MUSCAT GRAPES, OR PLUMS, OR FIGS, OR DRIED MORELLO CHERRIES

I now give you a simple grape pottage that is excellent. This is an easy period recipe that you can serve at a feast with the bread or without. By itself, it would not have much scope as a single dish entry in SCA Arts & Sciences, but if you made all of the fruit choices and made the bread from my first recipe in this cookbook you would then have an excellent entry. Please give it some consideration.

> **A FARE VNA SVPPA DI CIBIBO, O BROGNE, O FICHE, O** Marene Secche.
>
> PIGLIA Libra vna di Cibibo, e cauali l'anime, e lauale bene, e pos nilo in vna pignata con vn Bichiero di Vino dolce biancho, o Maluasia, e mes zo Bichiero d'acqua rosata, e libra meza di Zuccharo, e oncie quattro di Butstiero frescho, e vn pezzo di Canella, intiera, poi fallo bogliere quanto ti pare che basti, e habbi il tuo pane brustellato boffetto, in fettine quadre sottili, e ponilo nel fondo del piato, poi gettali sopra le frutta e sapore, e zuccharo, e Canella e similmente fa alle altre, e anche puoi imbandire senza pane, per variare, e in vece d'acqua rosa, puoi anche adoperare altra acqua.

Take a pound of Muscat grapes and remove the seeds, and wash well, and put them in a terra cotta pot with a glassful (~4 ounces) of sweet white wine or Malmsey, and a half-glassful (~2 ounces) of rose water, and a half-pound of sugar, and four ounces of fresh butter, and a whole piece of cinnamon. Then make it to boil as appears to be sufficient and get your toasted refined bread in square thin slices, and put them in the bottom of the platter. Then you shall cast over the fruit and sauce, and sugar and cinnamon, and in the same manner make with others. And also you can ready for the banquet without bread, for to vary, and instead of rose water, you can also use other water (like orange flower water).

Ingredients
1. ~9 Fresh figs (345g) (1 pound)
2. ½ Cup (115.2g) (of sweet white wine (4 ounces) (a Moscato would be good)
3. ¼ Cup (57.6g) of orange blossom water (2 ounces) (or rose water)
4. ¾ Cup (172.5g) of sugar (½ pound)
5. 1 Stick (115.2g) of butter (4 ounces)
6. A whole quill of true cinnamon
7. Several thin slices of refined white bread, toasted

Garnish
1. ½ Teaspoon of sugar on top per slice of bread and sauce
2. ¼ Teaspoon of ground true cinnamon on top per slice of bread and sauce

Redaction:

Place the first six ingredients in a medium, heavy bottomed pot and simmer for around 25 minutes or until the pottage is of the consistency that you like. Remove whole cinnamon stick and start toasting the bread slices. When this is done, take a plate or platter and place a slice of toasted bread in it and spoon some of the sauce over it and garnish each slice with sugar and cinnamon. You are done! This is a nice recipe for a feast as it is very simple and Christoforo says you can serve it without the bread if you want.

This is the only recipe where Christoforo says you can use something other than rose water, but if you want to substitute orange flower water for rose water in other recipes it would still be period practice.

Chapter 6

Sapori, Diversi Si Da Grasso Come Da Magro (Sauces Diverse as Well for a Day of Meat as Well for Lent)

42F   MUSTARD

Everyone loves good mustard and this recipe is very good and easy. It is a very rare occasion I have disagreed with a quantity of spice that Christoforo uses in his cookbook, but I think this mustard has too much ground cloves in it. There is a lot of clove used in this book, but usually does not give a recipe with a half-ounce of it.   Maybe he made a mistake or they made a printing error while publishing the book. If you cut this back, the mustard is very good.

MOSTARDA.

PIGLIA Libra vna di Zuccharo chiarificato, di Canella pesta fina oncia vna, di Cengeuro, oncia vna, di Garofani oncia vna [?], di seneua pesta oncie sei, et mescola ogni cosa insieme, e passa per lo setazzo, ouero macina ogni cosa insieme con vna macinella, e sera perfetissima, e non la volendo di Zuccharo li porrai del Mele.

Take a pound of clear sugar water, an ounce of fine ground cinnamon, an ounce of ginger, half-ounce of cloves, six ounces of ground mustard, and mix together, and pass through a sieve, or grind everything together with a handheld grindstone, and it is perfect, and if you do not want with sugar then you shall put honey.

Ingredients:
1. 1 and 1/3 Cups (345g) of clear sugar water or one cup of honey (1 pound)
2. 7 Tbs. (28.8g) of ground true cinnamon (1 ounce)
3. 5 Tbs. (28.8g) of dried ginger powder (1 ounce)
4. 3 Level tablespoons (14.4g) of whole cloves (Cut back to one or a half tablespoon, just too strong)(½ ounce)
5. 1 Cup (172.5g) of whole yellow or black mustard seeds (½ pound)

Redaction:

First make a simple sugar solution by taking a cup of sugar and pouring it into a small pan with a cup of water in it. Stir the solution and put it to the fire, bring to the boil and boil for 4 minutes. Cool the solution and measure out 1 and 1/3 cups and place in a bowl. If you want, you can use honey instead, just take a cup of honey and proceed with the recipe. Next, crush the mustard seeds and the whole cloves in a mortar and pestle or use a spice grinder. All of the spices need to be very well ground up. Add the spices to the cool sugar solution or honey and mix very well. I am thinking that you have to cut back on Christoforo's use of a half-ounce of ground cloves; it is just too strong. This mustard is used on roasted meats and sausages in the *Banchetti/Libro Novo*.

45A SWEET AND STRONG GREEN SAUCE

This is one of the first recipes I translated and is the first one I redacted. The tough part is figuring out the translation of the Italian word drago. I have some evidence in John Florio's Italian dictionary *Queen Anna's New World of Words* as the herb tarragon, but Emilio Faccioli in the *Arte Della Cuccina* says it is basil. With other uses I say it is tarragon, but I could be wrong, but either way the sauce is wonderful.

SALSA VERDE DOLCE, E FORTE.

PIGLIA Prasomeli, Menta, Drago, e pesta ogni cosa insieme, poi habbi mollena di pane piancho mogliata in aceto forte, e Sale, e Peuere, e distempera ogni cosa insieme, con aceto forte, E volendoli vn poco d'Allio potralsi porre, e volendola dolce, li porrai Mele, o Zuccharo.

Take parsley, mint, tarragon, (or basil) and grind everything well together. Then take crumb of white bread soaked in strong vinegar, with salt and pepper, dissolve everything together with strong vinegar, and liking it you can put a small amount of garlic and liking it sweet you shall put honey or sugar.

Ingredients:
1. ¼ Cup plus 1/8 cup of packed finely minced flat-leaved parsley
2. 1/8 Cup of packed finely minced mint
3. 1/8 Cup of packed finely minced tarragon
4. One slice of good white bread without crusts
5. 6 Tbs. of strong, good, wine vinegar
6. One clove of pounded garlic
7. ¼ Cup of honey
8. One Tsp. of salt
9. ½ Tsp. of freshly ground pepper

Redaction:

Soak the slice of bread in the vinegar for 20 minutes and squeeze out excess vinegar from the bread. Add all the other ingredients, and pound well in the mortar and pestle until well blended. If it is too sour, add more honey and if it is too sweet add more vinegar. This is very good on roast chicken, but goes well on all meats and fish.

45E WHITE, BLACK, GREEN AND YELLOW GARLIC SAUCE

I am a huge fan of the next sauce recipe because I very much love garlic. There are no set rules here, as Christoforo lets you decide on how much garlic to use or whether you want a thick or thin sauce and also what color you would like. You can even leave out the garlic and use ginger and pepper, which I have not done, but if you do it let me know how it turned out. I can't believe it will be better leaving out the garlic. The other thing is not to do the sauce with apricot kernels as this is just too dangerous as they contain cyanide. Maybe the kernels in the 16th century were not as bad as they are now. This is just wonderful on charcoal smoked pork butt!

AGLIATA BIANCHA, MORELLA, VERDE, E GIALLA.

PIGLIA i garugli delle Noci, e mondali, e mollena di pan bianco mogliata nel buon brodo, e Allio quanto ti piace, e Sale, e pesta bene ogni cosa insieme, poi distemperala con buon brodo, o di Carne, o di Pesce, secondo che ti piace e non li volendo allio, li porrai Peuere, e Gengeuro, e volendola Gialla, li porrai un poco di zaffrano, volendola Morella, o Incarnata, piglia carobbe, e rassale sottilmente, e ponle a bogliere in acqua, e cotte piglia la parte disopra che e colorita, e passala per la stamegna con brodo, e ponila in vna Pignatta, e falla leuare il boglio e distemperala con altro brodo, e passala per lo setazzo, e poi distempera la tua Agliata con piu colore, o meno, secondo che la vorrai aperta, o scura, le More al tempo farano tale effetto, e l'Vua nera. Similmente volendola verde, piglia i succo de Prasomeli, o Bieta, e lo porrai a bogliere in una pignatta con brodo, e Prasomeli, o Bieta, e come e ben cotta l'herba, e che e uenuto spesso, lo passerai per lo setazzo, poi distemperarai con brodo, e poi distemperarai la tua Agliata, e tal sapore va freddo, e in uece de garugli la puoi fare di Mandole, di Nizzole mode, e d'anime di Muniache, massimamente l'Estate, e si puote dare sola, o incorporata di viuande da Carne, o da Pesce allesso grosso, e sopra Macheroni.

Take the kernels of walnut and shell them and crumb of white bread soaked in good broth and garlic as much as you like, and salt, and pound all these things together well.

Then dissolve with good broth, or of meat or of fish, according to what you want, and if you do not want garlic you shall put pepper and ginger, and wanting it yellow you shall put a small amount of saffron, and wanting it brown or pinkish take carob carefully scraped and put them to boil in water, and cook, take the part on top that is colored and pass it through a cloth sieve with some broth and put it in a terra cotta pot and make it to simmer, and then dissolve with more broth. Pass it through a sieve and then paint your garlic sauce with more color or less according to whether you shall want light or dark, the mulberries in time shall make such like effect, and the dark grapes.

Likewise wanting it green, take the juice of parsley or chard, and you shall put it to boil in a terra cotta pot with broth and parsley or chard and when it has well-cooked the herbs and when it becomes thick you shall pass it through the sieve, then you shall dissolve with broth, and then you shall paint your garlic sauce.

And such sauces can be cold and instead of kernels you can make with almonds, with shelled hazelnuts, with seeds of apricots, especially in the summer, and you can set alone or use in foods of meat or of large boiled fish and over macaroni.

Ingredients
1. 1 Cup of walnuts
2. 3 or 4 Slices of good white bread without crusts
3. 1 Cup of good broth
4. 4 or 5 cloves of garlic or to your taste
5. ¾ Teaspoon of salt
6. Extra broth to your taste

Redaction:

Crumble the bread in a bowl and add the broth. Let it soak for 10 minutes, then squeeze the bread with your hands to remove excess broth. Pound the walnuts and the bread mixture with the crushed garlic and salt in a mortar or use a food processor. Do not over blend in the food processor or you will turn it into baby food! When it is mixed very well add extra broth to thin it out to your taste. I generally like it somewhat thick, but others like it rather thin—you are the judge. Notice that Christoforo also gives you the option of using different nuts such as almonds, hazelnuts and apricot kernels. Notice all the different colors he gives you, what fun! Christoforo says it can be used on macaroni. Sure would be doing some carbohydrate loading!

Chapter 7

Potacci, Brodi, E Robba In Tiella, & Pignata Stuffata, In Forno
(Pottages, Broths, and Things in the Pan and in the Terra Cotta Stew Pan and in the Oven)

50B CAPONS OR PHEASANTS IN POTTAGE OR OTHERS WITH THE BROTH UNDERNEATH

This next recipe starts us on the way for the cooking of all kinds of poultry. This one is very good, and notice how he wants you to add sour grape juice to add sourness to the dish. He tells you this because the raisins add sweetness so you use sour grape juice to balance out the taste. This is a very common practice in renaissance cooking and I think you will very much like the taste of this dish. This dish would make a nice main course for a large banquet. Also note that the recipe calls for prosciutto ham, but this is not the modern version, but a 16th century boiled ham with spices. Check out recipe 59E and you will see what I am talking about. The suggestions I give you are not what Christoforo wants, but are better choices than modern prosciutto ham.

CAPPONI, O FAGIANI IN POTACCIO O ALTRO, COLLA SVP, PA SOTTO.

PIGLIA Vn Cappone, o altro Vcello, e impillatalo bene, come fa, resti se uolessi farlo arrosto, e ponilo in un Vaso a bogliere sino che e quasi cotto Poi habbi vna Cazza di buon brodo con vna brancata d'Vua passa, e vna Noce moscata intiera, e un poco di Peuere, Canella, e Gengeuro pesti, e poco di Zaffrano, e ponili dentro detto Cappone a finire di cuocere, e un pochetto d'A grefto, si, che'l faccia acetoso, e Prasomeli, e un pochetto di Persutto per darli o s dore, Poi lo imbandirai in un piato, con fette di pane sotto.

Take a capon or other poultry and lard it well like you would make if you wanted to make it roasted, and put it in a pot and boil until so that it is half- cooked.

Then take a ladle of good broth with a handful of raisins and a whole nutmeg, and a small amount of pepper, cinnamon, and ginger pounded, and a small amount of saffron. And put it inside the named capon to finish with cooking, and a small amount of sour grape juice, so that it would be made sour, and parsley, and a small amount of ham (prosciutto) to give odor.

Then you shall ready it for the banquet in a platter, with slices of bread underneath.

Ingredients

1. 1 Capon or large stewing hen or chicken
2. 2 Tablespoons of good lard or bacon fat
3. Water to cover bird
4. Ladle of good chicken stock
5. 2/3 Cup raisins
6. 1 Whole nutmeg
7. ½ Teaspoon of freshly ground black pepper
8. 1 Tablespoon of ground true cinnamon
9. 1 Teaspoon of ground ginger
10. Pinch of ground saffron
11. ¼ Cup to ½ cup of sour grape juice (more or less)
12. 3 Tablespoons of minced country ham or good salt pork or jowl bacon
13. 3 Tablespoons of minced Italian flat leaved parsley
14. 4 Slices of good toasted white bread with the crusts removed

Redaction:

Place capon in a pot just big enough to hold it and just cover it with water. Add the lard and bring to the boil and partly cover the pot with a lid. Boil slowly for 30 minutes and then take a ladle of good chicken broth and place over the bird with the rest of the ingredients except the toasted bread. Then bring back to the simmer and finish cooking it say another 30 minutes or until done. Make sure the stock just covers the bird. When done, discard the nutmeg and check the broth for sourness. Add more sour grape juice if not sour enough. If you think there is too much broth, then remove the bird and keep warm while boiling the stock down for a while. When ready to serve, place toasted bread in a large deep platter and place the bird on top of the toast, then ladle some of the broth on top. You can also carve the bird and then place that over the toast then ladle over the broth. This is very renaissance looking!

50C   PHEASANT OR CAPON OR PIGEON OR BREAST OF VEAL OR OTHER MEATS STEWED IN THE TERRA COTTA POT IN THE OVEN

Here is another capon recipe that would be wonderful for a main dish at a large banquet. I think this is at its best cooked in a terra-cotta pot and, just like the recipe above, do not use modern prosciutto ham. I love the way they seal the pot with pastry dough, as this technique has been used thought-out medieval and renaissance times. Christoforo gives you many kinds of poultry and meats to choose from.

> FAGIANO, O CAPPONE, O PIZZONE, O PETTO DI VITELLO, O ALTRA CARNE TVFFATA
> in Pignatta, nel Forno.
>
> PIGLIA Il Fagiano, o altro, acconciato, e rifato, e ponilo in vna pignata con vn poco di Perfutto, o Carne falata, tagliata in fette, e Magiorana, e noce mofcata, e fucco di Naranci, e un poco di brodo, e Peuere ammaccato, e un poco di Zaffrano, e poi habbi fatto uno coperchio di Pafta fatto a pofta fopra detta Pignatta, et ponila nel Forno cofi ftoffata tanto che cuoca quello che li e dentro, Poi lo imbandirai, et vuole effere mangiato caldo, che, e Viuanda diuiniffima.

Take the pheasant, or others, dress and gut it and put it in a terra-cotta pot with a small amount of ham (prosciutto), or salted meat cut into slices, and sweet marjoram, and nutmeg, and juice of sour oranges, and a small amount of broth, and bruised pepper (corns), and a small amount of saffron. And then take a made covering of pastry made to position over named terra-cotta pot, and put this stew in the oven so much that cooks that which is inside. Then you shall ready it for the banquet, and wants to be eaten hot, which is the most divine food.

Ingredients
1. One capon or large stewing hen
2. 3 Tablespoons of chopped country ham or 3 or 4 slices of salt pork
3. 2 tablespoons of fresh minced marjoram or two teaspoons dried marjoram
4. ½ Teaspoon of freshly grated nutmeg
5. ½ Cup of sour orange juice
6. 1 ½ Cups of good chicken stock
7. 1 Teaspoon of lightly crushed pepper corns
8. Pinch of ground saffron

Redaction:

Place bird in a heavy, non-corrosive pot and add all of the rest of the ingredients, and place heavy aluminum foil on top with a lid that is weighted down with small rocks or small bricks to seal it tight. Bring pot to the simmer on top of stove, then place in a 325 degree F oven for around one and a half hours or until done. This would also be fun to do in a clay pot, as Christoforo suggests. To use a clay pot, soak the pot in water for 10 minutes then add the bird and the rest of the ingredients. Place lid on top and make a thick pastry with soft wheat flour and water and place it on the edge of the lid and seal very well. Place clay pot in a cold oven and turn temperature to 300 degrees F and heat for 15 minutes. Next, run temperature to 425 degrees F and bake it for around one and a half hours or until done. Serve it hot and it is very divine food indeed!

50E PHEASANTS, OR CAPONS, OR PIGEONS, OR BREAST OF VEAL, OR OTHERS COOKED IN SWEET WHITE WINE, OR VERNACCIA (THIS IS NOW A KIND OF DRY, WHITE WINE), OR MALMSEY, IN THE GERMAN STYLE.

Now I give you a fowl in the German style, which is one of my favorites. By itself this is a fairly easy dish to do, but if you wanted to enter this as a single dish in SCA Arts & Sciences, you could increase the scope of the dish greatly by making the prosciutto ham recipe in my cookbook 59E. This will take a lot of time and effort, but will show you how different 16th century prosciutto ham is compared to modern prosciutto ham.

FAGIANI, O CAPPONI, O PIZZONI O PETTO, DI VITELLO, O ALTRO COTTO IN
vino biancho dolce, o Vernazza
o maluagia, alla tedescha.

PIGLIA L'Vccello, e fallo cuocere in una Pignatta con libra meza di Persutto tagliato minuto in una delle sopradette sorti di Vino, con un quarto di Peuere intiero, e libra meza d'Vua passa monda, e poi piglia la mollena d'un pane brustolato in fette mogliate in aceto forte, e poi passale per lo setazzo, con aceto forte, et ponili libra meza di Zuccharo, e un quarto di Peuere pesto, e un quarto di Canella pesta, e un quarto di Gengeuro pesto, e un ottauo di Garofani pesti, e un poco di zaffrano tanto, che li dia il colore, E quando sera quasi cotto L'Vccello, o altra carne, li ponerai il sopradetto sapore, e lo finirai di cuocere.

Take the fowl and make to cook in a terra cotta pot with a half-pound of ham (prosciutto) cut finely in one of the above-mentioned kinds of wine, with one-quarter (ounce) of whole pepper, and a half-pound of seeded raisins. And then take the crumb of a toasted bread in slices soaked in strong vinegar, and then pass through the sieve with strong vinegar, and put a half-pound of sugar, one-quarter (ounce) of pepper pounded, and one-quarter (ounce) of ground cinnamon, and one-quarter (ounce) of ginger pounded, and one-eighth (ounce) of cloves pounded, and a small amount of saffron, so much that it gives the color.

And whenever the fowl are half-cooked or other meats, you shall put over it the named sauce, and you shall finish with cooking it.

Ingredients

1. One capon or large stewing hen
2. Minced country ham (175.5g) (6 Ounces)(salt pork and jowl bacon will work, as well)
3. 1 Bottle of white sweet wine (Sutter Home Moscato)
4. ¾ Tablespoon (7.2g) of whole pepper corns (¼ ounce)
5. 1 ¼ Cups (172.5g) of raisins (½ pound)
6. 4 Slices of toasted good white bread with the crusts removed
7. ½ Cup of strong red wine vinegar
8. ¾ Cup (172.5g) of sugar (½ pound)
9. ¾ Tablespoon (7.2g) of ground black pepper (¼ ounce)
10. Heaping tablespoon (7.2g) of ground true cinnamon (¼ ounce)
11. Heaping Tablespoon (7.2g) of ground ginger (¼ ounce)
12. 1 ½ Teaspoons (3.6g) of ground cloves (1/8 ounce)
13. Pinch of ground saffron

Redaction:

Place fowl in a large, non-corrosive pan and add ham and wine, whole peppercorns, and raisins. Make sure fowl is just covered with liquid, use extra wine or water if needed. Bring to the boil, turn heat down and simmer fowl for 20 minutes with the pan partly covered with a lid. While the fowl is cooking, crumble the toasted bread in a bowl, add the wine vinegar and mix well. Soak for ten minutes, and push the mixture through a metal sieve or loose cheese cloth. You will need more liquid to do this, so you can use more vinegar, but after you have sieved it, press out excess vinegar with your hands. When the toast vinegar mixture is sieved, add the sugar and spices, and mix very well. When the 20 minutes is up, add this mixture to the pan with the fowl and mix very well. Bring back to the boil and simmer for another 20 minutes or until the capon is done. Taste the liquid and balance out the sweet/sour flavor, more sugar if too sour and more vinegar if too sweet.

51A BRAIN OF VEAL, OR CAPON, OR BREAST OF VEAL UNDERNEATH (A SAUCE), OR OTHERS

The next recipe is another capon dish that I think is very good. This one has got it all: fruit, spices, garlic, herbs and pork lard. This one would make a spectacle on a banquet table. I hope you are not too upset that I choose capon rather than the brain of veal. I also added a lot of garlic; you can cut this back if you want.

TESTA DI VITELLO, O CAPPONE O PETTO DI VITELLO
sottostato, o altro.

PIGLIA la Testa del Vitello pellata bene biancha, e dagli un boglio buono. Poi mettila in vna Tiella con Lardo pesto, ouero Dileguito, e ponila nel forno, ouero sopra le bragia a soffrigere da ogni banda, che venga colorita, poi li ponerai vn poco di brodo con Brogne, Marene, e spigoli d'aglio, e Ramelle di Finochio, poi pigliarai vna mollena di Pane brustolata in fette, e mogliata in agresto, pestata nel mortaio, e passata per la stamegna, metendoli dentro d'ogni sorte di specie peste, e getterai ogni cosa sopra la Testa nella Tiella, e herbe oliose pi stazzate, e farai bogliere tanto che sia cotta, e la imbandirai in vn piato, gettando li sopra il sapore, e ogni cosa che e nella Tiello.

Take the brain of veal skinned very white and give a good boil, then put in a pan with pounded lard, or oil, and put it in the oven, or over the coals, to fry on every side, so that it becomes brown, then you shall put a small amount of broth with prunes, cherries and cloves of garlic, and stalks of fennel.

Then you shall take a crumb of toasted bread in slices and soak it in sour grape juice, pound in the mortar and pass it through the cloth filter, placing inside it every kind of pounded spice, and you shall cast everything over the brain in the pan, and pounded herbs in oil, and you shall make to boil so much that it is cooked and you shall ready it for the banquet in a platter, casting over it the sauce and everything that is in the pan.

Ingredients:

1. Capon (7.36 avoirdupois pounds)
2. 4-5 Tablespoons of pork or bacon fat
3. 16 Cups of water or enough to cover capon in the pan
4. Heaping cup of pitted prunes
5. Heaping cup of pitted cherries (I used a three variety blend)
6. 6 Cloves of peeled garlic
7. Heaping cup of fennel stalks (use white bulb part only)
8. 3 Slices of toasted, good white bread without crusts
9. 1 Cup of sour grape juice
10. Spices to wit: teaspoon of ground true cinnamon, a teaspoon of ground ginger, a ½ teaspoon of ground black pepper, a ¼ teaspoon of ground cloves, a teaspoon of salt
11. Herbs in oil to wit: a tablespoon of pounded basil, a teaspoon of pounded thyme, a tablespoon of pounded sage, a teaspoon of pounded rosemary, all mixed with a tablespoon of olive oil.

Redaction:

Remove capon from packing and remove the giblets. Rinse in cool water and place in a heavy bottomed pan just large enough for it to fit, toss in the giblets without the liver and add enough water to cover. Cover the pan and bring to the boil, remove cover and boil slowly for 20 minutes. When time is up, carefully remove capon from the pan and let drain, but keep the broth. Let everything cool a bit. When cool, dry off the capon very well with a towel. If you let it stay in the water to cool, it will overcook and you cannot do the other steps.

Next, take your toasted bread without crusts, tear apart in a bowl and soak in the sour grape juice for 15 minutes. When bread is soaked, squeeze out excess sour grape juice with your hands and pound the pulp in a mortar and pestle or whiz in a food processor for a while until it is very sticky. Filter the pulp through cheesecloth (I used a brand called Pure Acres Farm unbleached cotton cheesecloth that I thought worked very well) using around 5-6 cups of the capon broth to help wash it through the filter. Squeeze out all the juice you can from the pulp and discard what is left on the cheesecloth.

Next, take the pork fat and heat very well in a large skillet and, when very hot, place capon bottom side down and brown it for around two-three minutes, then carefully place it on the breast side and brown it also for 2-3 minutes. Next, brown the other side the same way. When it is browned and cool enough to handle, place the capon back into the pot you boiled it in and add the broth you filtered through the cheesecloth, should be around 5-6 cups, and add the prunes, cherries, garlic, and fennel with the spices and herb in oil and bring to the boil, cover and simmer for around a 20 minutes or until the capon is done. If the legs jiggle in their sockets it is done or check the breast with an instant read thermometer, should be done at 170 to 180 degrees. Next, take a large platter and carefully place capon in the center, spoon the fruits and vegetables over it and spoon the sauce over it. A dish worthy of a Duke of Ferrara!

52A   TO MAKE CAPONS, OR PHEASANTS, OR YOUNG FOWL, OR PIGEONS IN SAVOY CABBAGES, OR TURNIPS, OR LETTUCES, OR ONIONS

This is the last capon dish I have redacted from this chapter and, as you can see, a very versatile one as there are many vegetable choices. I used onions, but the savoy cabbage also looks very good. It is very interesting that they half roasted the fowl and then cooked it with the vegetables to finish cooking it, a very 16th century way to do it. I would be very surprised if a modern palate disliked this dish.

A FARE CAPPONI, O FAGIANI, O POLLASTRI, O PIZZONI IN
Verze, o Nauoni, o Lattuche, o Cipole.

PIGLIA i Coresini delle Verze, o Lattuche, ben netti, e lauati, e tagliati in quarto, e ponili a cuocere in buono brodo grasso, con un buono pezzo di Persutto, e vna buona pestata di Lardo, e prasomeli tagliati minuti. Poi habbi i tuoi Vcelli quasi cotti, e ponli a finire di cuocere in dette Verze, i Nauoni tagliarai minuti in fette, e le Cipole in quarto seruando l'ordine del resto, che s'e detto nelle Verze, o Lattuche. Auuertendoti che nele Verze, o Lattuche, sono molto buoui gli Vcelli bene impillotati, e piu che mezo cotti arrosto; poi bisogna finirli di cuocere allessi in dette Verze, o Lattuche, e fra gl'altri la Anadra saluatica, e Pizzoni casalenghi, li sono molto buoni.

Take the hearts of the savoy cabbages or lettuces, well cleaned, and washed and cut into quarters, and put it to cook in good rich broth, with a good piece of ham (prosciutto), and a good pinch of lard, and parsley finely minced. Then take your half-cooked fowl and put it to finish cooking in named cabbages, the turnips you shall cut in very small slices, and the onions in quarters, attend to the order of the rest that is named in the cabbages or lettuces.

Note that the savoy cabbages, or lettuces, are very good when the fowl is well larded and more than half-roasted cooked, then you need to finish with cooking by boiling with named savoy cabbages or lettuces, and among the others the wild duck and the domestic pigeons are very good.

Ingredients:
1. 3 Medium white onions, quartered
2. 4 ½ Cups good strong chicken stock (I used Costco chicken broth with a pinch of Minor's chicken base)
3. 4 Ounce chunk of country ham
4. 2 tablespoons of pork lard
5. 1 bunch of Italian parsley, chopped (leaves only)
6. 1 Small hen (I used one about 5 pounds)

Redaction:
Take the hen and dry it very well and place three strips of bacon on top of it and roast it for one hour in a 350 degree F oven. Then take the first five ingredients and place in a pot and bring to the simmer, cover, and simmer for 30 minutes. When the fowl is done, remove the bacon and place the fowl in the broth, making sure that it is just covered with liquid. Add more water or broth if you need to. Simmer for 20 minutes or until the fowl is done. This recipe is very modern to the taste and surprising good.

Chapter 8

Robbe Per Antipasti, O Tramezi, Come Polpette, Cervellti, Salciccie, Dobbe, & Altre Simili, Come Disotto Appare
(Things for the Beginning of the Feast, or Middle of the Feast, Like Meat Rolls (or Meatballs), Brain Sausages, Sausages, Pickled Meat in Sauce, and Similar Others, That Appear Below)

54C SAUSAGES ON THE SPIT

This recipe is a sausage that is very good. When Christoforo talks about a spit he means an iron rod which can have spikes fitted to it to hold meat on the bar or a cage to hold meat on the bar. The bar is placed on iron prongs on the side of the iron fire structure. You can simplify this recipe by making patties and let them stand overnight in the fridge and then frying them in a little olive oil or pork fat. When they are done, soak in the stewing ingredients for a few minutes and these would be very good for a banquet. I would also encourage you to wrap them in caul fat and roast over a fire or grill them on a charcoal grill.

TOMASELLE NELLO SPIEDO.

PIGLIA Carne di vitello, o castrone, o porco magra da i Coscetti, e nettala bene da i nerui, e pellegate, e pestala bene con i coltelli có un poco di Lardo, e grasso di Vitello, et herbe oliose, et dopoi che sera ben pesto ogni cosa insieme con i coltelli, con Torli d'Voua e Formaggio grattato, e specie miste, secondo la quantita che vorrai fare, hauerai rete di Porco, o Vitello, e gliele inuolgerai dentro come hai fatto le altre, e le farai grande, o picciole come vorrai, poi le porrai a cuocere nello spiedo colle steche, e come serano cotte le attuffarai in vna Pignata con zucchara, e Canella, e succo di Naranci, e vogliono essere mangiate calde.

Take meat of veal, or wether (castrated sheep), or lean pork from the leg, and clean it well from the sinews and skin, and pound it well with the knives with a small amount of lard, and fat of veal, and herbs in oil. And then when it shall be well pounded everything together with the knives, with egg yolks, and grated cheese, and mixed spices according to the quantity you shall want to make, you shall have in position caul fat (omentum) of pork or veal, and in it you shall wrap inside (the mixture above) like you have made in the others, and you shall make them large or small like you shall want. Then you shall put to cook on the spit with bars (or splints) (or a cage) and when they are cooked you will stew in a terra cotta pot with sugar, and cinnamon, and sour orange juice, and it is intended for this to be eaten hot.

Ingredients (sausages):
1. 2 Pounds (690g) of lean veal, lamb, or pork
2. 4 Tablespoons of good lard
3. Herbs in oil to wit: 1 tablespoon of minced fresh basil, 1 tablespoon of minced fresh oregano, 1 tablespoon of minced fresh rosemary mixed with 1 tablespoon of good olive oil. Any fresh herbs will be alright.
4. 2 Egg yolks
5. 4 Tablespoons of grated parmesan cheese
6. 1 Teaspoon of ground true cinnamon
7. 1 Teaspoon of salt
8. 1 Teaspoon of ground black pepper
9. 1 Teaspoon of ground fennel seeds

Ingredients (stewing):
1. 3 Tablespoons of sugar
2. ½ Tablespoon of ground true cinnamon
3. ½ Cup of sour orange juice

Redaction:
Grind the meat in a food processor or meat grinder, or chop finely with a sharp knife and pound in a mortar and pestle if you want to do it the way it was done in Christoforo's time! When all the meat is ground, add all the sausages ingredients and mix everything together very well. Next, take sections of caul fat and stuff with the meat mixture, you can make them large or small as you wish but it is easier to cook them when they are smaller. You can get caul fat (omentums) from a good butcher shop or google it on the internet. When they are all wrapped, tie them with string or a strip of caul fat. Next prepare a small charcoal fire and grill the

sausages on all sides slowly until nice and brown. Should take around 20 or so minutes if they are not too large. When they are done, place in a covered pot and add the mixed stewing ingredients and let soak for a few minutes.

56F   LOIN OF BEEF IN THE GERMAN STYLE

This recipe I called *Banchetti* beef and was one of my favorites. Beef in 16th century Italy was considered one of the poor cuts because it was too expensive to raise in quantity. What is interesting about this is that it is also why you see so much veal, they slaughtered the young cow as soon as it was about to start eating grass i.e. milk fed veal. What beef they used was from cattle that died or were very old. Notice that Christoforo tells you to beat the loin and then soak it in vinegar; this is to make the meat more tender. They are cooking it just like the recipe above on a spit, but now they have a dripping pan under the cooking roast to catch the drippings along with a place to put some of the soaking liquid. Christoforo knew what he was doing back then!

LOMBO DI BVE ALLA ALEMANA.

PIGLIA Il lombo di Bue grasso, ch'abbia del frolo, e nettalo bene da quelle pelegate, e Nerui che ha atorno, poi battilo molto bene e ponilo ammoglio in Maluasia, e Aceto, ma piu aceto, con poluere di Coriandoli, e Finochi, e poco Sale, e lasciaglielo per spacio di cinque in sei hore. Poi ponilo ad arrostire nello spiedo, e come e ben cotto ponilo in vno piato, ma mentre si cuoce, poni nella giotta vn poco di quello Aceto, e Maluasia, doue e stato ammoglio, e posto che lo ha uerai nel piato ponili sopra detto sapore, che ponerai nella giotta con quello che se ra collato del Lombo, e coprilo, e lascielo attuffato cosi meza buon'hora. Dopoi sera perfettissimo.

Take the loin of fat beef, that you would get from the lean, and clean it well from the skin and sinew that are all round about. Then beat very well and put to soak in Malmsey wine, and vinegar, but more vinegar, with ground coriander, and fennel, and a small amount of salt, and leave for the space of five or six hours.

Then put to roast on the spit, and when it is well cooked put in a platter. While you cook, put in the dripping pan a small amount of that vinegar and Malmsey wine which remains from soaking. And place what you have in the platter, putting over named sauce that you put in the dripping pan with those that are drippings from the loin, and cover, and leave things to soak a good half-hour. Then it shall be perfect.

Ingredients:
1. 5 Avoirdupois pound chuck roast (other cuts will work as well)
2. 3 Cups of sweet red wine (Elysium is what I used)
3. 4 Cups of good red wine vinegar
4. 2 Tablespoons of ground coriander seeds
5. 1 Tablespoon of ground fennel seeds
6. 2 Teaspoons of salt

Redaction:
Place wine in a non-corrosive container, mix well all of the rest of the ingredients and pour over the beef roast. Cover roast and let marinate for six hours or overnight in the fridge. Make sure roast is covered with the marinade. Remove roast from the marinade and dry it very well. Place it on a cookie sheet and bake for 15 minutes in the oven at 450 degrees F, and then turn down oven to 325 degrees F and bake for 1 ½ hours or until done. While the roast is cooking, simmer the marinade in a non-corrosive pot for an hour or so. Taste and see how sour it is and if it is real sour add a little bit of sugar to balance it out. When roast is done, let it rest for 15 minutes and then place in a covered bowl, add a few ladles of the cooked marinade and let it stew for a half hour or more. It also would be fun to brown the

roast on all sides a bit over charcoal then place off to the side in the smoker that is not over the coals. Place a non-corrosive pan over the coals with some of the marinade in it, close the smoker lid and smoke it for a couple of hours or until done. Then let roast cool a bit and then place in a covered pot with some of the cooked marinade from the smoker pan and let stew as above. It is now perfect indeed!

Chapter 9

Gelatie Diverse
(Diverse Gelatins)

57E   TO MAKE EGG WHITE GELATIN IN THE FRENCH MANNER FOR TEN PLATTERS

This next one is a very spectacular gelatin recipe, which is very laborious and expensive, but what a sight to see when it is done. This is one of the very few recipes that use long pepper and grains of paradise. Note the use of egg whites to clarify the gelatin and make it translucent. This is a dish fit for the high table to honor the Duke and the Cardinal. If you try this redaction, you must e-mail me and tell me how it turned out.

A FARE GELATIA CHIARA
Francese per piati dieci.

PIGLIA Vn bocale grande di Vino biancho, et se sera dolce, sera migliore. Piglia poi piedi quattro di Vitello, e quattro Cigotelli di Vitello, cioe le menature de i ginocchi, e cauane tutte l'ossa, e poi lauale a piu lauature, poi poni a bogliere la Carne una buon'hora, e come, e ben cotta la carne cauala fuori e colla col setasso la decottione, poi habbi libra vna e meza di Zuccharo, e oncia vna e meza, di Canella, e di Garofani vn terzo, di Noci moscata un qninto, di Zaffrano, un terzo di Peuere longo un quarto, e uncia meza di Grani paradisi, ogni cosa pistassato, e il biancho, d' Voua dieci bē battuti, e vn Bichiero d'aceto biancho forte, e poni ogni cosa a bogliere nella Decottione, e come ha bolito vn poco, ponila nella cassa a collare per due volte, ponendoli pero sempre il conueniē te Sale, e sera buonissima.

Take a large bottle (1.385 Liters x 1.5 my best guess) of white wine, and if is sweet, it is better. Take then four feet of veal, and four small legs of veal, to wit the joint of the knee, and remove all of the bone and then wash with much washing. Then put the meat to boil for a good hour, and when it is well cooked, remove them outside, and strain the decoction with the sieve. Then take one and a half- pounds of sugar, and one and a half- ounces of cinnamon, and a third- (ounce) of cloves, one- fifth (ounce) of nutmeg, one- third (ounce) of saffron, one quarter- (ounce) of long pepper, and a half-ounce of grains of paradise, everything ground, and the whites of ten eggs well beaten, and a glassful (~4 ounces) of strong white vinegar, and put everything to boil in the decoction, and when it has boiled a little, put it twice through the sock sieve, whereupon always putting suitable salt, and it is excellent good.

Ingredients:
1. 2 1.5 Liter bottles of Sutter's Home Moscato white wine
2. 6 Veal feet
3. ~5 Cups of water
4. 2 ½ Cups (517.5g) of sugar (1½ pounds)
5. 9 ½ Tablespoons (43.2g) of true cinnamon (1 ½ ounces)
6. 1 Teaspoon .(76g) of ground nutmeg (1/5 ounce)
7. 2 Tablespoons plus one teaspoon (9.6g) of ground cloves (1/3 ounce)
8. ~2 Tablespoons (9.6g) of saffron (I only used a ½ tablespoon (2.4g) because of the expense (1/3 ounce)
9. 1 ½ Tablespoons (7.2g) of ground long pepper (Piper longum)(¼ ounce)
10. 2 ½ Tablespoons (14.4g) of ground grains of paradise (Aframomum melegueta)(½ ounce)
11. 10 Well beaten egg whites
12. Scant ½ cup (100.8g) of white wine vinegar (I used Monari Federzoni with a 7% acidity)(4 ounces)
13. 2 Teaspoons of salt

Redaction:

I placed the veal feet into a five gallon pot and added both bottles of wine and added the water until they were covered with liquid, around five cups. I covered them and brought to the boil, then removed the top and boiled the feet for one hour. I did not remove the meat from the bone as Christoforo says, as I did not have the knees, but used extra veal feet.. It is also easier to remove the meat after they cook. The translation seems to indicate boiling the meat instead of the bones, but if you want a gelatin you have to include the bones! I am sure he meant to boil both the meat and the knees. I then removed the feet when cool and sieved the wine solution with a large linen sock filter. Next I added all the spice ingredients to the wine solution and mixed them in well. Note that the saffron will grind more easily if you grind it with the salt; beat the egg whites until they are frothy and turn white and add to the wine solution. Boil the wine solution for 10 or 15 minutes and cool a little. I then sieved the solution through the linen sock filter, but I would recommend a looser material like cheese cloth and in period they would have had loosely woven linen that would have been just like cheese cloth. I then sieved it a second time through a linen filter. I noticed that the first filtering is very difficult if you don't use a loose filter, as the egg whites are clarifying the solution of all the spent spices, which makes a lot of sieved material on the cloth. It is also a good idea to have a place to hang the sieve and let it drip, as the work becomes very laborious and time consuming, as I found out Next, I took the cooled wine solution and poured it into two kinds of molds. My gelatin was brown colored because I don't think I was able to sieve it properly, and I think it should be a very intense red or yellow color (especially if you use all the saffron Christoforo wanted) that is somewhat clear. I am very disappointed that Christoforo did not tell me more of how to present it, but I had some guidance from other gelatin recipes.

You can add the boiled meat from the legs and knees (or use other boiled veal or chicken meat) to the bottom of the mold with, say, some fresh laurel leaves to make it attractive. The way to do this is to add a small amount of the cooled wine solution to the molds and place in fridge until it gels. Then add your laurel leaves and meat in an attractive pattern and add the rest of the wine solution and place the molds in the fridge for some time. Unmold by dipping the top of the mold in warm water then placing a nice looking platter on top of the mold and turn it upside down and the gelatin should come right out.

Chapter 10

A Fare Salami
(To Make Preserved Meats)

59C SAUSAGES

I now give you a delightful sausage recipe, which I redacted many years ago. Christoforo gives almost all the ingredient amounts except the quantity of beef you need. Over thirty-eight pounds of pork and a piece of beef. It looks like to me the beef ratio to pork was very low so my amount of beef in the recipe is way too high. Once you mix the ground beef and pork, you take a pound of that and add the rest of the ingredients, which puts them in the right proportions. This turns out very well, but will be somewhat salty, as you need a high salt content to preserve the sausage.

> SALCIZZONI.
>
> PIGLIA Pesi due di Carne di Porco, e pez'vno di Carne di Māzo, e pesta bene ogni cosa insieme, e per ogni libra di Carne, li porrai oncia meza di Sale, e grane sei di Peuere ammaccato, e un poco di Finochio a tuo giuditio, e spugneza bene ogni cosa, poi inuestirai queste cose, e fa che siano ben calcate in budelle di Manzo lauate, e curate, come le altre sopradette.

Take two pesi (38.2 avoirdupois pounds) of meat of pork and a piece of meat of beef, and pound everything together well, and for each pound of meat, you shall put a half-ounce of salt and six grains of bruised pepper, and a small amount of fennel seed as you judge, and sponge everything well, then you shall invest (or stuff) these things, and make that they are well pressed in washed intestines of beef, and cure, like the others above-named (recipe 59A).

Ingredients (1/10 recipe):
1. Lean pork (690g) (2 pounds)
2. Lean beef (345g) (1 pound)
3. Mixed pork and beef fat (345g) (1 pound)
4. 24 Bruised peppercorns
5. 48 Bruised fennel seeds
6. 3 Tbs. plus one tsp. (57.6g) of salt (2 ounces)
7. Several feet of 35mm to 38mm natural ox casing

Redaction:
Pound chopped meats and fat in a mortar and pestle or put them through a meat grinder and add peppercorns and fennel seeds that have been coarsely broken up in the mortar. Add salt and mix everything very well. Wash out your casings if they are in salt and pat them dry. Stuff the casings with a sausage horn or use the sausage attachment on the stand mixer, making sure there are no air pockets in the sausages. Tie them every six or eight inches with kitchen twine and when they are all done prick them all over with a pin and hang in a cool well ventilated (I used a fan) room (or just use the fridge) for eight days. These would be very good to smoke cook in a charcoal grill or you can just grill them in a frying pan or over charcoal. These will also freeze well uncooked.

59E TO MAKE PROSCIUTTO (ITALIAN HAM)

Now I give you the 16th century version of prosciutto ham. This one is a lot of time and work, but also a lot of fun. One of the jobs I hated was deboning the pork legs, but if you have a good butcher you might get him to do it. If this is an Arts & Sciences entry, you need to do it yourself. This makes a great single dish entry; I know because I have done it. As I have told you before, this is going to be a much different ham from modern prosciutto ham, as you can see from the technique and the ingredients. The finished product will last a long time and you can freeze small portions to use in other period recipes.

A FARE PERSVTTI.

PIGLIA i Coffetti de Porci di pefi otto, in dieci, e ponili in Sale, e ogni due giorni fregali colle mani molto bene, e come hanno bene prefo il Sale, ca uali fuori di quella falamora, e fogliono pigliare il Sale in giorni Vinti tre. Poi pi glia vno Caldaio di Vino biancho, o nero, e fallo bogliere, e piglia i Perfutti ad vno ad vno, e cacciali in detto Vino bogliente, efcabuzzali cofi tre, o quattro volte, e mettili da canto ad vno ad vno, e poi ritorna anchora da capo a fare il fi mile, e quefto farai fei uolte per cadauno. Dopoi mettili fopra una Tnuola difefi e poi piglia libra una di Coriandoli ben pefti, e inuolgerai in detta poluere i Per futti, e poi li metterai in foppreffo fra due affe, e quando ferano ftati vn tempo cofi, pigliarai libre due di Coriandoli ammaccati, e libr' vna di Finochi, e oncie tre di poluere di Garofani, e li coprirai di dette cofe, e poi li ritornarai vn'altra volta in foppreffo, per due altri giorni, e poi li cauarai difoppreffo, e li poncrai ad afciugare in luoco caldo, ma doue non fia troppo fuoco, e ferano perfettiffimi.

Take the hind legs of pigs of 152.8 to 191 avoirdupois pounds, and put them in salt, and every two days rub them with the hands very well. And when they have taken well the salt, remove them outside this brine, and they are accustomed to take the salt in 23 days.

Then take a cauldron of white wine or red, and make it to boil, and take the hams one by one and plunge them in named boiling wine, swap them so much as three or four turns and place them by the side one by one, and then return again by the top to do them likewise. And this you shall do six turns for each one. Then place them over a table length, and then take a pound of coriander well pounded and envelop the hams in named powder.

And then you shall place them to press between two planks, and when they are in this state for a while, you shall take two pounds of bruised coriander (seed), and one pound of fennel (seed), and three ounces of powder of cloves, and you shall cover with named things.

Then you shall return them another time to the press for two more days, and then you shall remove them from the press, and you shall put them to dry in a hot room, but where there is not too much fire. And they are most perfect.

Ingredients (¼ recipe):
1. 38.2 Avoirdupois pounds of whole fresh pork hind legs (two legs)
2. Forty to fifty pounds of kosher salt (more or less)
3. 15 Liters of red wine (I used a dark red Franzia in the box)
4. 2 3/4 Ounces of ground coriander seed
5. 5 ½ Ounces of bruised coriander seed
6. 2 ¾ Ounces of bruised fennel seeds
7. 2/3 Ounce of ground cloves

Redaction:
Take pork legs and remove the bones trying to keep the meat in one piece as much as possible. Leave the fat and rind on the legs. I put them to the salt in a cooler, but I used one that was a little too small, so use one that

is big enough to hold all the salt that needs to surround them. I also used a cooler so I could control the temperature of the curing process, as I did not have a cool room or a root cellar to cure them in. I used a small block of blue ice to keep the temperature in the low fifties just like in a root cellar. I took around 10 to 12 pounds salt (this may vary according to your cooler size) on the first day and rubbed it well into all the cavities of the meat (this is very important) and then covered the meat in salt all around. I then added my blue ice block and closed the cover on the cooler with a sticky note noting the day's date. After two days, I removed the legs from the salt and threw away all wet salt. I then rubbed fresh, dry salt into all the cavities and returned them to the cooler, with dry salt all around the meat. This first two day period will be the most water you will pull from the meat, and each two day period after it the amount of water will decrease. Keep up the routine for 23 days, as Christoforo instructs and, at the end, as he says 'they will take the salt'. Keep replacing wet salt and rub in dry salt as well as you can, and keep the temperature down, and you will have no problem of them spoiling. On the 24th day, remove them from the salt and rinse under cold water and start your wine to boiling (I used a 10 gallon pot). Add pork legs carefully to boiling wine and bring wine back to the boil (this may take a while). When they come to the boil move them around in the pan with a large paddle or spoon every now and then, and boil for 15 to 20 minutes. Carefully remove them from the boiling wine, dry them very well with a clean towel, and dust them with the ground coriander seed. Christoforo says to place them between two wooden planks for a while. My method was to place them in a towel lined cookie sheet, one on the bottom and one on top inside a cooler. I also added some weights to the top cookie sheet to help press out excess moisture from the hams and to form them up. I added a small blue ice block to the cooler to lower the temperature, as I was doing this in the middle of summer. Check on them every day as they need to be kept as dry as possible, changing the towels as needed. I went for four days in this stage, as Christoforo says a while, this was my best guess. Remove the pork legs from the cooler and dust them well with the powdered cloves, bruised coriander seeds, and the bruised fennel seeds. At this stage, it might be nice to wrap them in cheese cloth, as all these spices make quite a mess every time you move them. Return them to the cookie sheets in the cooler for two more days, keeping them dry and weighed down. After two days, remove legs from cooler and place them on a cookie sheet in a very low oven (say 150 to 200 degrees F) for an hour or so. You are going for drying, not cooking. You can also lower the oven temperature by placing a pot holder in the door so that it does not get too hot. Cool them, and if they are not already wrapped in cheese cloth you want to do so now. They will last a long time in a root cellar, or the fridge, or you can freeze them, and as Christoforo says 'they are most perfect'.

Chapter 11

Trattati Di Pesce
(Treatises on Fish)

60C FRESH AND SALTED MUSHROOMS IN VARIES WAYS

This next recipe is everything you wanted to know about fixing renaissance mushrooms. I give you Variation One and Five. It is very interesting at the beginning of the recipe on how to remove the poison from the mushrooms, which will not work. In general, the Italians knew which ones to pick that are not poisonous, but obliviously they did not understand all of the problems you can run into. You had better know what you are doing if you pick them fresh from the field.

FONGI FRESCHI, E SALATI, A VARII MODI.

PIGLIA i tuoi Fongi freschi, e tagliali in quarti, se son grandi, e metti li a bogliere in acqua con mollena di pane, e Allio, per cauarli il veneno, poi falli scolare bene da l'acqua, e ponli in un Vaso con vn poco d'Olio buono, e Sale, e Prasomeli, e menta molto ben pesta, e soffrigi ogni cosa pianamente, poi piglia acqua, & Agresto ch'habbia dello acetoso, e mettine ne i detti Fongi, tanto che ti paia ch'habbia del chiaro, e dello spesso, poi falli bolire molto bene per mez'hora e ponili dentro Peuere, Canella, Gengeuro, Sale, e Zaffrano, tanto che ti paia che stian bene, e vn poco di Mele, o zuccharo, tanto ch'habbi un poco del tenero, e metti dette robbe quando boglione, e starano bene.

Ad'altro modo, li mondarai, e ponerai a cuocere nella Tiella, con Olio, Peuere, e Sale.

Ad'altro modo, li porrai a cuocere nella Tiella con Lardo, Sale, e Peuere, e Allio pestato minuto co i Coltelli.

Ad'altro modo, dopoi che hanno boglito, e che son purgati, frigeli nella patella, con Naranci, Peuere, e Sale sopra.

Ad'altro modo. Pigliarai i fongi infarinati, e fritti, e li porrai in vna Patella con Allio, e Prasomeli pesti minuti con i coltelli, e Olio buono, e Agresto, o succo di Naranci, e Peuere, e soffrigerai ogni cosa insieme con sale, seran buoni, e cosi si potra conciare i Fongi salati, facendoli stare quattro hore in acqua tepida, e seruare l'vltimo modo. Eccetto che non li metterai Sale.

Take your fresh mushrooms and cut them in quarters, if they are large, and put them to boil in water with the crumb of bread and garlic to remove the poison. Then make them to drain well from the water and put them in a pot with a small amount of good oil, and salt, and parsley, and mint pounded well a great deal, and fry everything gently.

Then take water and unripe grape juice that would have some sourness, and place with the named mushrooms, so much that you see that they have of the thin and of the thick (in other words add enough water and unripe grape juice to make it neither too thin nor too thick). Then make to boil very well for a half-hour, and put inside them pepper, cinnamon, ginger, salt, and saffron, so much that you see that they are good, and a small amount of honey or sugar, enough that they would have a little softness, and put named things when boiling and they shall be good.

In another way, you shall clean them and you shall put them to cook in the pan with oil, pepper, and salt.

In another way, you shall put them to cook in the pan with lard, salt, and pepper, and garlic pounded very small with the knives.

In another way, after they have boiled, and when they are purged, fry in the flat pan with sour orange juice, pepper and salt on top.

In another way, you shall take the lightly floured mushrooms and fry and you shall put them in a flat pan with garlic and parsley pounded very small with the knives, and good oil, and sour grape juice, or juice of sour oranges, and pepper, and you shall fry slowly everything together with salt, they shall be good. And like this you can cure the salted mushrooms, making them to stand four hours in tepid water and serve them in the last way, except you shall not put salt.

Variation 1

Ingredients
1. One pound (avoirdupois) of regular button mushrooms
2. Four cups of water (or to cover)
3. 3 Tablespoons of good olive oil
4. ¾ Teaspoon of salt
5. 4 Tablespoons of minced Italian parsley
6. 2 Tablespoons of minced mint
7. ¼ Cup of water
8. ¼ Cup of sour grape juice
9. Spices to wit: ¼ Teaspoon of pepper, ½ teaspoon of ground true cinnamon, ½ teaspoon of ground ginger, pinch of ground saffron
10. ¼ Cup of honey

Redaction:
   Take the mushrooms and place in a large pot with the four cups of water, make sure they are just covered with water. Boil slowly for three minutes and drain. Heat oil in a medium frying pan and add mushrooms, salt, parsley and mint, and fry slowly for two or three minutes. Add the rest of the ingredients and boil slowly for half an hour (you may need to add more water by tablespoons if it gets too dry), ready to serve. Sweet and sour mushrooms, most excellent!

Variation 5

Ingredients

1. One pound (avoirdupois) of regular button mushrooms
2. One Tablespoon of soft wheat flour
3. 4 Cloves of crushed garlic
4. 3 Tablespoons of minced Italian parsley
5. 3 Tablespoons of good olive oil
6. ¼ Cup of sour orange juice
7. ½ Teaspoon of ground black pepper
8. ¾ Teaspoon of salt

Redaction:
   Boil the mushrooms in water, as stated above, and drain. Toss the drained mushrooms with the flour and mix well. Heat oil in a frying pan and add the rest of the ingredients and fry slowly for half an hour. You may need to add water by tablespoons if it dries out too much. This is a very good dish with the garlic and sour orange and oil. I put a lot, you can cut it back if you want.

66D TO MAKE PEA PODS FOR A DAY OF MEAT AND LENT

There is archeological evidence that humans were eating wild field peas as early as 9,700 BCE. I googled the word ervile in the Italian from the *Banchetti* and guess what, I got a whole lot of information on different types of peas. Some things just don't change over time. Both the meat and Lenten versions would be very aggregable to modern taste.

> A FARE RVVIA IN TEGOLE,
> da Graſſo, e da Magro.
>
> PIGLIA le Tegole della Ruuia tenere, e tagliali via il fiore e il picolo, e ponila a cuocere in buon brodo graſſo, con un poco di Perſutto tagliato minuto, minuto, per darli odore. Poi le imbandirai, e li porrai ſopra vn poco di Peuere, e queſto e quanto a i di da graſſo, e per li giorni da magro la cuocerai in'acqua con Buttiero freſcho, e vn poco di marzolino tagliato minuto, o altro Forsmaggio buono.

Take the pods of tender ervile peas, and cut them by the flowers and the stalk, and put it to cook in good rich broth, with a small amount of prosciutto ham cut very finely to give it odor. Then you shall ready them for the banquet and you shall put over them a small amount of pepper, and this is when it is a day of meat.

And for the day of Lent you shall cook them in water with fresh butter, and a small amount of fresh sheep cheese* cut very small, or other good cheese.

* Marzolino – A fresh sheep cheese made in March, hence the name.

Ingredients (day of meat):
1. 2 and 2/3rds cups (Six avoirdupois ounces) of snow peas or any immature pea pods
2. 3 Cups of good broth (I used Kirkland brand chicken broth)
3. 2 Generous tablespoons of minced country ham or salt pork or jowl bacon
4. ¼ Teaspoon of ground black pepper

Redaction:
Simmer the chicken stock with the minced country ham for ten minutes to make sure the ham is cooked. The ham in period would be already cooked, and our country ham is closer to the period ham than modern prosciutto ham is. Next add your snow peas, bring back to the boil and boil for five minutes or until done, but do not overcook. Drain the pea pods from the broth and add the black pepper. I also added a ¼ teaspoon of salt as the period ham was very salty. Mix them well and you are ready to serve the dish.

Ingredients (Lenten day):
1. 2 and 2/3 cups (Six avoirdupois ounces) of snow peas
2. 3 Cups of water
3. ½ Stick (four ounces) of butter
4. ¼ Cup of minced sheep cheese (I used a young Spanish Manchego)

Redaction:
Bring the water and butter to boil in a small pot and add the peas. Bring back to the boil and simmer for five minutes. Drain the pea pods

from the liquid and place in a small bowl and toss them with the cheese. Dish is now ready to serve. I never thought I would say this but the Lenten dish is better than the meat dish!

67A   STRESSED TURNIPS, FOR TEN PLATTERS

If you don't like turnips, this is the recipe for you. Almost anything will be good if you put enough butter and cheese on it, and boy does Christoforo do it. If you want to cook them in butter instead of roasting them, it looks like he wants you to peel them and I would add that you cook them in ghee (butter with no milk solids i.e. clarified butter). This method is definitely more expensive.

RAPE SFORZATE, PER PIATI DIECI.

PIGLIA Rape numero trenta, e falle cuocere in libre tre di Buttiero e poi tagliale in fette sottili, et habbi di Formagoio grasso, libre cinque medesima mente tagliato in fette sottili, et habbi una Teggia, e ponili dentro un suolo di rape, e vno di Formaggio, e di Buttiero libre tre, di Zuccharo libre due, di Canella oncia vna e meza, e vn quarto di Peuere tramezo a tati suoli, quanto vorrai, e poi le farai cuocere co'l testo, ponendoli quando seranno cotte altro Zuccharo, e Canella, e Buttiero fresco disfatto sopra, e non potendo, o non volendo fare tanta spesa, Cuocerai le Rape arrosto nelle bragie, e dopoi le mondarai, e le farai in fette, et ancho le potrai fare in piatelli d'Argento, ma sono migliori nelle Tegiette di terra ben vidriata, e mettine vna picciola per piatello.

Take turnips numbering thirty, and make to cook in three pounds of butter, and then cut them in thin slices. And get five pounds of rich cheese likewise cut in thin slices. And get a pan and put inside a layer of turnips, and one of cheese, and three pounds of butter, of sugar two pounds, of cinnamon one and a half-ounces, and a quarter (ounce) of pepper between to all layers as you shall want. And then you shall make them to cook in the mobile terra cotta (or metal) oven, putting when they shall be cooked other sugar and cinnamon, and fresh melted butter over, and cannot or don't want to make a lot of expense, you shall roast cook the turnips on the coals, and then you shall peel them, and you shall make them into slices. And also you can make them in small platters of silver, but it is better in the well-glazed terra cotta pot, and put with them a small quantity per small platter.

Ingredients (1/4 recipe):

1. 8 Medium turnips
2. 1 and 1/8 Sticks (259.2g) of melted butter (9 ounces)
3. 3 ¼ Cups (432g) of shredded provolone cheese (15 ounces)
4. ¾ Cup (172.5g) plus 1 tablespoon plus 1 teaspoon of sugar (6 ounces)
5. 2 Tablespoons (10.8g) plus 1 teaspoon of ground true cinnamon (1/3 ounce)
6. 1 Teaspoon (1.8g) of ground black pepper (.06 ounce))

Redaction:

I chose to roast them, so place the turnips on a layer of cookie sheets (so as not to burn the bottoms of the turnips) and place in the center of a 350 F degree oven for two hours. Take the turnips out and let cool a bit. Peel the turnips with a sharp filet knife, sometimes the peel will pull off and sometimes you will have to cut it off, not a pleasant task! When they are peeled, cut them into thin slices. Take a 13x9x2.5 inch baking pan (I used Pyrex glass) and place a layer of sliced turnips in the bottom and add some melted butter, some sugar, pepper, cinnamon, and some shredded cheese. Layer these ingredients until all the ingredients are used up, but finish with cheese on top. Place dish in the center of a 350 degree F oven and bake for 45 minutes. Remove from oven, let stand a bit, and serve. What a decadent turnip dish! Everyone will eat their turnips now. Christoforo says to garnish the top with more sugar, cinnamon and butter, but I don't think it needs it. If you want to, sprinkle a tablespoon of sugar, a tablespoon of melted butter and a half teaspoon of cinnamon.

68D TO MAKE ONIONS IN THE FRYING PAN

This next recipe is very interesting in the technique used to cook the onions. Boil them first until nearly done, and then flour them and brown them in a frying pan with butter. Leaving them whole makes a nice presentation, which they dearly loved in the renaissance. Ground pepper for a garnish on the onions but no suggestion of placing sugar or cinnamon. This one is the rare exception.

A FARE CIPOLLE IN TIELLA,

PIGLIA Le tue Cipolle, e mondale, poi falle alleſſare in'acqua intiere pero, e quando ſerano cotte, le farai ſcolare dall'acqua, e poi le infarinarai, e le porrai in vna Tiella con buon'Olio, e le farai frigere, ponendoli vn Teſto diſopra, ſiche venga ben colorite, e poi le imbandirai, ponendoli ſopra un poco di Peuere, & in vece dell'Olio, le potrai frigere in Buttiero freſcho, e ſerano migliori.

Take your onions and peel, then make them to boil in water still whole. And when they shall be cooked, you shall make them to drain from the water, and then you shall flour them, and you shall put them in a frying pan with good oil. And you shall make them to fry, put a covering on top, so that they become well colored. And then you shall ready them for the banquet, putting over them a small amount of pepper, and instead of oil you can fry them in fresh butter, and they shall be better.

Ingredients:
1. Four medium white or red or yellow onions
2. ¼ Cup of soft wheat flour (more or less)
3. ½ Stick of butter (more if needed)
4. ¼ Teaspoon of ground black pepper (or more)

Redaction:

Take the onions and peel them, but do not cut off the top or bottom, as you want them to stay together while boiling in the water. Place them in a medium sized pot that will just hold them without stacking them. Cover the onions with water to just covering them, and bring to the boil on top of the stove. Bring them to a simmering boil for one hour or until done. It is a good idea to have another pot with simmering water nearby to add more boiling water to the onion pot when it gets low. Drain the onions carefully into a strainer, as you don't want to break them apart. Let them sit for a while to cool a bit and then cut the head and tail off then place them on a plate and flour them well all around.

Next get an iron or heavy bottomed frying pan and place on a top burner with the butter and bring the butter to a hot temperature. Carefully place the floured onions in the hot butter and cover the pan. Use a low flame as you want browning not burning. Brown for five minutes and move the onions to brown on another side, keeping the cover on the frying pan. Repeat this operation for a total of four times in order to brown all the sides as well as you can. Carefully remove the onions to a serving plate and sprinkle the pepper over them and you are done. I love onions, so this is a big hit for me!

68E   TO MAKE FRIED GOURDS

The next recipe deals with one of the oldest food crops, the gourd. They have been found in archeological digs as far back as 13,000 BCE. Even today, there is a lot of taxonomic confusion about what a gourd is and what a squash is. The one we are interested in is the Lagenaria siceraria gourd, which comes in all kinds of sizes and shapes just like squashes. Squashes are all new world crops and their genus and one of the most common species is Cucurbia pepo. Try growing some gourds, for they are amazing on how fast they grow and how tall of vine they produce.

A FARE ZVCCHE FRITTE.

PIGLIA Le Zucolle tenere, che non siano molto grosse e, poi che le bauerai rassate, le tagliarai in fette sottili; e le distenderai, gettandoli sopra del Sale, tanto che pigliono vn poco detto Sale, poi le frigerai in Olio, o in Buttiero, se condo che vorrai, ma infarinandole pero prima, e poi che serano fritte, le imbandirai, ponendoli sopra Finochi freschi sgranati, e Agresto.

Take tender gourds that are not very large, and then when you shall have peeled them, you shall cut them in thin slices and you shall spread them, casting over them the salt, enough that they take a small amount of named salt. Then you shall fry in oil or in butter, according to what you shall want, but flouring them however first. And then when they are fried you shall ready them for the banquet, putting over them fresh grated fennel and sour grape juice.

Ingredients:

1. Two medium zucchinis (or 8 six inch gourds)
2. One teaspoon of salt (or more)
3. ¼ Cup of soft wheat flour (more if needed)
4. 4 Tablespoons of olive oil (more if needed)
5. 3 Tablespoons of grated fresh fennel
6. 3 Tablespoons of sour grape juice

Redaction:

Slice the zucchini into ¼ inch rounds (if using gourds you need to peel them and then slice). Lay the slices out on a cookie sheet and scatter half the salt on them, turn them over and scatter on the rest of the salt. Let the slices sit for 15 minutes and then pat them dry with a cloth or paper towel. Next take the slices and lightly flour both sides, the easiest way to do this is to place the flour on a plate and dip each side into the flour, knocking off excess flour. Heat the olive oil in a large skillet and add the slices carefully to the hot oil and fry for 3-4 minutes on each side, or until lightly browned. Do not crowd the pan, so you will have to do them in stages. When they are done, drain on a paper towel. When all are fried, place them on a serving tray and sprinkle over the sour grape juice and garnish with the grated fennel. This is a very popular dish!

68F TO MAKE FRESH BEANS IN THE POD

The next recipe is beans in the pod and what kind of bean were they eating in the *Banchetti*? I think the likely answer to that was Vigna unguiculata, commonly known as the black-eyed pea. I think they could have eaten the immature black-eyed pods as we would eat green beans, Phaseocus vulgaris. I did not have any black-eyed pea pods, so I redacted the recipe with modern green beans. If you wanted to make this recipe authentic, grow some black-eyed peas and enter it in a A&S event. That would be very cool.

A FARE FASOLETTI FRESCHI IN TEGOLE.

PIGLIARAI Le Tegole de Fasoletti quando sono tenerini, e ta gliarai il picollo, poi le porrai a cuocere in'acqua bogliente, e subito si cuoceranno, et cotte che serano, le porrai a scolare col Sale sopra, poi le frigerai in Olio, ouero Buttiero, e frigendole nella patella, li porrai vn poco d'Aceto, e Peuere, e poi le imbandirai.

You shall take the pods of beans (black-eyed peas) when they are tender, and you shall cut them small, then you shall put them to cook in boiling water, and they shall cook quickly. And when they shall be done you shall put to drain with salt over, then you shall fry them in oil or butter, and frying them in the pan, you shall put a small amount of vinegar and pepper, and then you shall ready them for the banquet.

Ingredients:
1. 8 Cups (one avoirdupois pound) of green beans cut into 1 inch lengths
2. 1 Teaspoon of salt
3. 4 Tablespoons of olive oil
4. 4 Tablespoons of cider vinegar (or red wine vinegar)
5. ½ Teaspoon of ground black pepper

Redaction:

Take your green beans and cut a little of the stem off and wash in cold water. Drain well in a colander and cut them into one inch lengths with a knife. Take a large pot of boiling water and add the green beans to it and bring the water back to the boil. Boil five minutes and drain the beans in a colander very well.

While the green beans are draining, heat the olive oil in a large skillet. When the beans are drained carefully add them to the hot oil with the salt and sauté them gently for five minutes. When the time is up, remove from heat and add the vinegar and pepper. They are now ready to serve to the Duke!

Note that in period, they would be using young tender pods of black-eyed peas. As far as I can tell, Christoforo wants these beans to be al dente (to the tooth) as the French still do.

Chapter 12

Latticini
(Milk Products)

70B TO MAKE A COMPOTE OF RIND OF MELONS, OR RIND OF GOURDS, OR TURNIPS, OR WHOLE UNRIPE PEACHES, BY PRESERVING FOR LENT

This next recipe would be the 16th century's equivalent of fine dining. This is a whole lot of time and work, but I wanted you to see what they thought was a special dish. I loved the fact that they wanted you to put it into an ornamental decorated vase. This is a very special dish indeed.

A FARE COMPOSTE DI SCOZE DI MELONI, O SCOCIE, O ZVCCHE, O RAPE,

ouero Persiche integre e acerbe, da cóseruare, per Quaresima.

PIGLIA La quantita delle sopradette cose, secondo il tuo parere, e mondale, e ponele ammoglio nell' Aceto con Sale per quindici o venti giorni. Dopoi le cauarai dell' Aceto, e le ponerai in vn vaso con acqua, & li darai vn buon buolio, e poi le cauarai e le gettarai in vn'altro vaso d'acqua fresca, & ge le lasciarai tanto che siano raffredate. Poi le cauarai di dett'acqua, & le distenderai sopra vn'Asse, mettendoli dopoi vn'altra Asse disopra con pesi che le sopressino, & le lasciarai cosi in soppresso per vn giorno. Pigliarai poi vn vaso, & ge le metterai dentro, con tanta Sabba che dette Robbe stiano coperte, e le farai fare vno buon boglio in detta Sabba, di modo pero che non si disfaciano, e le ponerai in vna Orna acconciatamente, & li gettarai sopradetta Sabba doue haranno bolito, & ge le lasciarai cosi per venti giorni. Dopoi pigliarai vn'altro vaso, & le cauarai di detta Orna, & ge le metterai dentro con Mele, e Sabba, e Canella, Peuere, e Gengeuro, e Zaffrano, secondo la quantita che vorrai fare, e cime d'Osmarino, & Saluia, & farle ribolire un'altro poco con le sopradette cose. Poi tornale in sopradetta orna col detto sapore, e serano fatte. Et se non ti graua la spesa, fara bolire questa ultima uolta in Mele solo.

Auuertendoti che le Persiche non uano soppressate.

Take the quantity of the above-mentioned things according to your wants, and peel, and put to soak in vinegar with salt for fifteen to twenty days.

Then you shall remove it from the vinegar, and you shall put it in a vessel with water, and you shall give it a good boiling, and then you shall remove it and you shall place it in another vessel of fresh water, and you shall leave it so much that it would be cooled. Then you shall remove it from named water, and you shall spread it over a board, then putting over it another board with weight that presses, and you shall leave this in a press for a day.

You shall take then a pot, and with it you shall put inside with enough cooked grape must that named things would be covered, and you shall make it do a good boiling in named cooked grape must, in a way however that does not break it apart, and you shall put it in an ornamental decorated vase (or pan), and you shall lay over it named cooked grape must which has been boiling, and you shall leave this for twenty days. Then you shall take another vase, and you shall remove it from named decorated vase, and you shall put it inside with honey, cooked grape must, and cinnamon, pepper, ginger, and saffron according to the quantity that you shall want to make, and tips of rosemary and sage, and make to re-boil another bit with the above-mentioned things.

Then return it to the above-mentioned decorated vase with named sauce and they are done, and if you do not deepen the expense, you shall make to boil this last time in honey alone.

Notice that the peaches do not want to stay suspended.

Ingredients:

1. 1 Honeydew melon
2. 1 Quart of red wine vinegar (I used Pompeian)
3. 2 Tablespoons of salt
4. ~8 Cups of water to boil in
5. ~8 Cups of water to refresh in
6. Two 3 Quart bottles of Welsh's 100% grape juice
7. 1 ½ Cups of honey
8. 1 Cup of cooked grape must (sapa)
9. 1 Tablespoon of fine ground true cinnamon
10. 1 Teaspoon of fine ground black pepper
11. 1 Teaspoon of ground ginger
12. Pinch of saffron threads
13. 1 Tablespoon of minced fresh rosemary
14. ½ Tablespoon of minced fresh sage

Redaction:

Take the honeydew melon and peel it, split it in half and remove the center seeds and pulp, remove the flesh from the rind and eat or save it for another time. Next cut the rind into three or four inch pieces and place in a non-corrosive container and add the well mixed salt and vinegar to the rind pieces. Place a good lid on it and let marinate for fifteen to twenty days. I let it marinate for twenty days in a cool dark place, but not the fridge.

When the time is up, remove the rind pieces from the vinegar salt mixture and place in a non-corrosive pot with eight cups of water or enough to cover them, and simmer for 30 minutes. Simmer or boil slowly, as you do not want to break the rind pieces apart. When ready, carefully remove the rind pieces and place them in another pot with eight cups of cool water and let cool completely. Remove the rind carefully and place on a large cutting board or cookie sheet and place another board or cookie sheet on top. Add some weight (I used around thirty pounds). This will press out excess water from the rind and you will need towels to clean it up. Let stand like this for 24 hours.

Make the grape syrup (sapa) by placing the grape juice in a large heavy duty pot and simmering for three or more hours or until it is a syrup consistency. The best pot for this is tin-lined cooper, but enamel coated cast iron will work, but near the end you will have to stir it a lot to keep it from burning or scoring. You should have enough sapa for the marinade and for the last boiling. Remove the rind from the press and add to a non-corrosive pot and cover the pieces with the cooked grape must and simmer slowly for 30 minutes. When done, place the rind and grape must in a non-corrosive container with a good lid and place in a cool dark place for twenty days, but not the fridge.

When the time is up, carefully remove the rind from the marinade sapa and place in a non –corrosive pot with ingredients 7-14 and give it a ten minute simmer and let it cool. You can now place it in a fancy vase as Christoforo says, if you have one. This will keep for a long time in a cool dark place, but will keep longer in the fridge. This dish would make a wonderful entry for single-dish cooking in A&S. This tastes better than you think and the sauce is to die for!

IL FINE
(The End)

Bibliography

The Sansoni dictionaries, English-Italian, Italian –English, edited by Vladimiro Macchi, Third edition, 1988

Sansoni-Harrap Standard Italian Dictionary, volumes 1-4 1990 ISBN 0 24559635-6

Queen Anna's New Word of Words, or Dictionarie of the Italian and English tongues, Collected, and newly much augmented by John Florio, London 1611

Arta Della Cucina, Libri Di Ricette Testi Sopra Lo Scalco Il Trinciate E I Vini Dal XIV AL XIX Secolo. A cura di Emilio Faccioli. 1966

The Gourd Book by Charles B. Heiser Jr., 1979 ISBN 0-8061-2572-1 (paper)

About the Author

Mr. Potter has been cooking for over 50 years and his favorite cuisines are French, Mexican, and Italian Renaissance. He is a Cooking Laurel in the Society of Creative Anachronism and resides in a wonderful Manor in Lexington, Kentucky with his black cat Panther. He helps support Clouded Leopards through World Wildlife Fund for Nature.

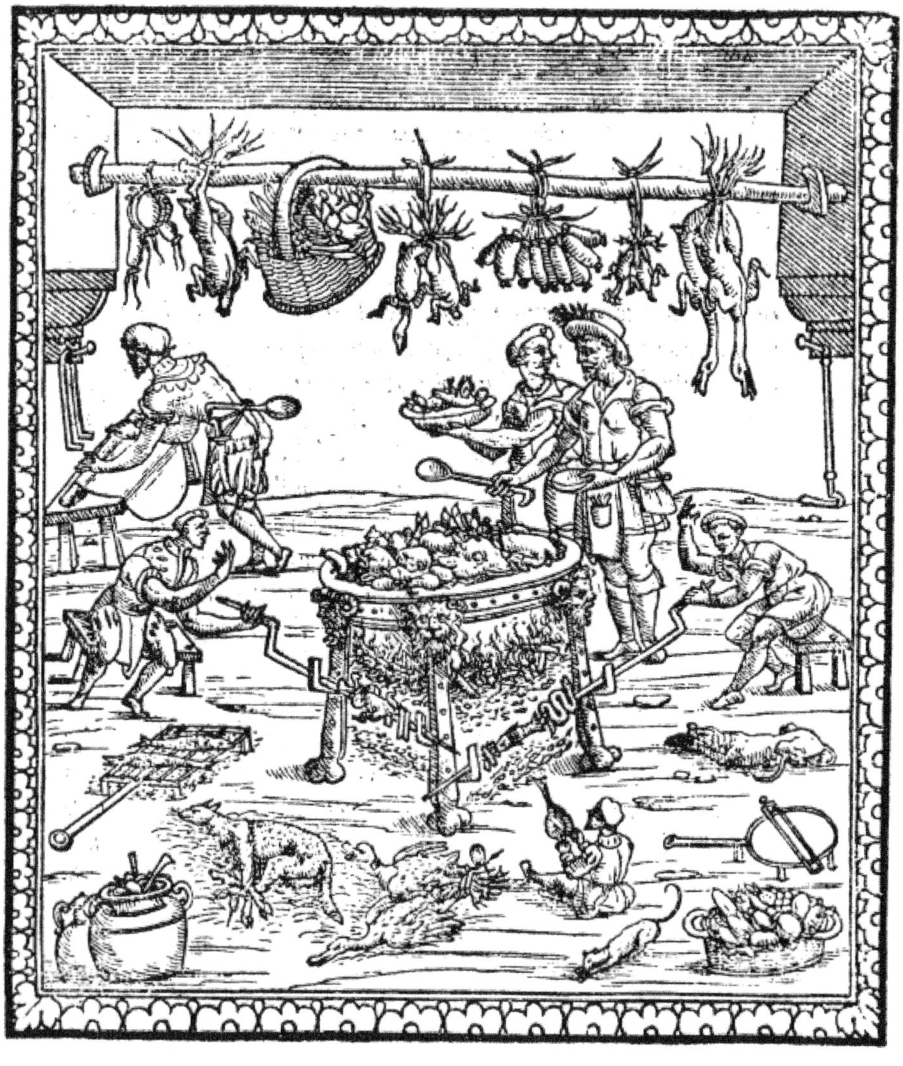

BANCHETTI

Printed in Great Britain
by Amazon